No Sugar—No Visible Fats—

Absolutely Vegetarian

A COMPLETE GUIDE TO MAINTAINING A STRICT
VEGETARIAN LIFESTYLE!

Lorine Tadej

TEACH Services, Inc.
Brushton, New York

ISBN: 0-945383-92-4
Library of Congress No. 94-60720

Cover art and design by Bill Newman.

Published by:
TEACH Services, Inc.
Route 1, Box 182
Brushton, New York 12916

Table of Contents

Why Be a Strict Vegetarian?[*]

Please read the information at the beginning of this book, before using the recipes. It will help you to maintain your good health or restore health, if you have lost it.

God wants you to be happy and healthy and has provided the essentials.

[*]See article *Do You Need a B_{12} Supplement* on page 137.

Letter From the Author

Dear Friend:

These recipes were compiled or invented or adapted with loving care. Please forgive the human errors.

I enclose a prayer for good health.

Food should look good, taste good and be good.

Who but God could have planned so perfectly in His diet for His people?

"In grains, fruits, nuts are to be found all the food elements that we need."[1]

"Grains, fruits, nuts and vegetables constitute the diet chosen for us by our Creator. These foods, prepared in as simple and natural a manner as possible, are the most healthful and nourishing."[2]

"Five hours at least should elapse between each meal and always bear in mind that if you would give it a trial, you would find that two meals are better than three."

"The first education children should receive from the mother in infancy should be in regard to their physical health. They should be allowed only plain food, of that quality that would preserve to them the best condition of health, and that should be partaken of only at regular periods, not more often than three times a day, and two meals would be better than three."[3]

"Life is a gift of God. Our bodies have been given us to use in God's service and He desires that we shall care for and appreciate them. Our bodies must be kept in the best possible condition physically, and under the most spiritual influences, in order that we may make the best use of our talents."[4]

"The things of nature are God's blessings, provided to give health to body, mind and soul."[5]

"Those who accustom themselves to proper exercise in the open air, will generally have a good and vigorous circulation. More people die for want of exercise than through over fatigue; very many more rust out than wear out."[6]

"Many a mother sets a table that is a snare to her family.... The mother should study to set a simple yet nutritious diet before her family."[7]

"Our sisters often do not know how to cook.... It is your duty to teach your daughters to cook."[8]

"Some of you send your daughters, who have nearly grown to womanhood, to school to learn the sciences before they know how to cook, when this should be made of the first importance."[9]

"Food should be prepared with simplicity, yet with a nicety which will invite the appetite... Let all who sit down at your table see upon it well-cooked, hygienic, palatable food. Eat regularly, and eat only food that is free from grease..."[10]

"Grains and fruits prepared free from grease, and in as natural a condition as possible, should be the food for the tables of all who claim to be preparing for translation to heaven."[11]

(Webster defines 'grease' as an oily matter...)

"The free use of sugar in any form tends to clog the system and is not infrequently a cause of disease."[12]

"The less of sweet foods that are eaten, the better; these cause disturbances In the stomach and produces impatience and irritability In those who accustom themselves to their use."[13]

"God will work wonders for us if we will in faith cooperate with Him. Let us, then, pursue a sensible course, that our efforts may be blessed of Heaven, and crowned with success."[14]

Why should we eat so simply? Why should food be eaten in its original form as much as possible? Why eliminate free fats? Why eliminate sugar? Why whole grains? Why avoid refined proteins?

There is really only one reason and it is very simple. God's diet for man. Do you believe God knows what He is doing? Does He balance proteins, fats, sugars, starches, vitamins, minerals, fiber content, etc., in His food?

God meant for us to eat apples; not just drink the juice and throw the rest away. The combined parts, as balanced in peanuts and kernels of corn, are what our bodies need. We do not need the squeezed-out free fats saturating our foods.

God made us and God made food, so He knows whole grains have what we require in correct proportions, so leave the bran, etc., where it belongs.

Oh, that poor misunderstood protein! If we eat it in the natural state as found in nuts, grains, legumes, etc., our body uses it as God planned. Please leave it in the bean and in the kernel.

We need oil, so get it from olives, not olive oil. Avocados, nuts and many foods have oil in correct proportions.

We need natural sugars, but all we need is in God-given fruits. We thank God for the knowledge and pray good health for all.

With warm wishes for healthful, happy, tasty cooking.

Lorine Tadej

1. CDF 92, 2. MH 296, 3. CDF 228–229, 4. CH 49, 5. CH 169, 6. CH 173, 7. CDF 236, 8. CH 144, 9. CH 149, 10. CDF 354, 11. CDF 355, 12. CDF 197, 13. CDF 321, 14. CH 172 (Complete Titles listed on pg. 33)

Basic Questions and Answers

1. What shall we eat?

   Fruits, vegetables, nuts, grains, legumes, daily. As close to whole and natural as possible.

2. What is a balanced meal?

   A. Fruit Meal:

   Cereal or bread
   2 or 3 fruits
   Nut butter or Fruit-nut butter

   Use 2 or 3 fruits with whole grain breads or whole grain cereals. Using fruits in season keeps costs down, but you can freeze or can or dry fruits to be used all year. Many fruits do not need sweetening, but if they do, use apple juice or pineapple juice. These are the grains you can use as cereals:

   Millet (whole or meal)
   Barley
   Rice (brown or wild)
   Wheat (whole or cracked)
   Corn (coarse or fine meal)
   Oats (steel cut or oatmeal)
   Rye (mix with others)

   If you have your own mill, grind grains just before cooking, as cereal or in other recipes. A combination of grains is better in breads and cereals than wheat alone. (*See CDF p. 321*)

   B. Vegetable Meal:

   Protein dish or protein vegetable combination
   Variety of vegetables (cooked or as relishes or as salad)
   Potatoes are excellent food

   Potatoes are a wonderful food—use them! Use several vegetables at a meal. They may be combined in a soup or stew or salad, or be served separately. Use grains, legumes or nuts, or combinations of these. If family members are active, good whole-grain breads can be served at all meals, too.

3. Is it attractive?

   Use to advantage color, texture, taste. Do not over cook food, especially fruits and vegetables. Crisp foods should be crisp.

Soft foods should be soft. Chewy foods should be chewy. Use a variety of several tastes, colors and textures in the meal.

4. How much does it cost?

Garden produce is not free, but it is fresh and foods 'in season' save. Are the items in regular use? Do you have to make a special trip to a store? Are the high-cost ingredients essential to taste or nutrition? Can you substitute? Is the cost relative to the dietetic value? Is it a special occasion? Are the ingredients 'junk' or food? PLAN! PLAN! PLAN! Make a week's menus at a time. You will save if you plan.

5. Do I have the ingredients?

Keep your staple stock always up-to-date. (Herbs, seasonings, freezer items, canned goods, packaged items.) Store the newest in back. Stagger shopping so you do not run out of everything at once.

6. How long will it take to prepare?

Good food is vital, but meal planning and preparation should not take all day. If one recipe takes a lot of time, let other menu items be simple. Plan a complicated dish for a day when you have extra time and energy.

7. Can it be prepared in advance?

Use dry containers for granola and zwieback. Make a double recipe so you can freeze some. Make a dish ahead that keeps in the refrigerator.

8. Will leftovers freeze to become a new dish?

Freeze leftovers for future, or several days' 'dabs' may be a casserole or soup. Save liquids, too. Juices can be combined. Use your imagination.

9. Do I think about energy conservation?

Use your oven to full capacity. Appliances that shut off automatically when temperature is reached are savers. Top of the stove cooking is the most wasteful.

10. What is the food value?

Consider all the ingredients of a recipe to determine over-all nutrition. Most pasta has no food value. Use sauces on rice, barley, beans or whole grain bread. Think, dear friend, "Is this food 'cheap,' or inexpensive?" Use a variety of fruits and vegetables and grains every day. Only food that is eaten feeds the body, so make your food tasty and attractive to your family. A stew or soup or salad can be a meal. Serve it with whole grain bread.

11. What about salt?

Taste your combined ingredients BEFORE adding salt. Always start with half the amount suggested in the recipe. If you need any, it takes less if the salt can be added to already hot food. Adding a little lemon juice may make salt unnecessary.

Use a low salt product like Pa Pa Dash. It can be purchased at a regular food store. Better yet, use Bragg's Liquid Aminos, it can be purchased at health food stores. Liquid Aminos can also be used where ever a recipe calls for soy sauce.

Non-Irritating Herbs

Anise seed

Basil

Bay leaf

Caraway

Celery seed

Coriander

Cumin

Dill seed

Fennelseed

Garlic

Mace

Marjoram

Mint

Onion

Oregano

Paprika

Parsley

Poppy seed

Rosemary

Saffron

Sage

Sesame seed

Tarragon

Thyme

Turmeric

Try these in small amounts until you see
how your family likes them.

Introduction

This information will help you to reach your ideal weight and maintain it, as long as you live.

Adam and Eve were an ideal weight because they ate food, as God gave it to them, in a natural state.

You can follow God's food plan today and you will be amazed, as I was, at how easily you can reach and keep your perfect weight.

Tell your family that you do not want to hear the word diet. To start with; a diet is a temporary weight loss plan and this program is for life.

After I had lost about 25 or 30 pounds, the praise did help. Fatties need support in words and actions. Thanks so much to those who really helped!

As a fatty, I knew all the tricks and deceptions.

As soon as I was alone, I started to eat. I also ate in the night because no one was watching. I hid junk food in my own dresser drawers.

All of this helped my meals to seem a sensible size.

Until I had fully accepted the present plan for my life, I just got very busy at the times food would be the greatest temptation. I have never been hungry once on this program.

Getting every bit of junk food out of the house helped a lot and I have never felt deprived.

Please write if I can help in any way. *We all* need help sometimes. I want everyone who reads these pages to have a "Newstart."

N—nutrition
E—exercise
W—water
S—sunshine
T—temperance
A—air
R—rest
T—trust in God

I have written about each of these factors to show how they have helped me to reach my ideal weight and have maximum health.

Nutrition

I, Lorine Tadej, challenge you to follow this plan for 30 days and then to follow it all of your days.

You can do anything for one month, can't you, dear friend?

One doctor has said, "There are built-in safety factors in the natural food that God provided for us, that prevent us from becoming obese. On a natural diet where no sugar or visible fats of any kind are added to the diet, obese patients will lose weight, even though they are eating all that they want."

Fruits and vegetables do not digest at the same rate, so it is best to have 2 vegetable meals and 1 fruit meal or 2 fruit meals and 1 vegetable meal.

Use natural, unrefined foods only and always. Do not allow between meals eating ever.

Have regular meals 5 to 5½ hours apart 7 days a week. Very rarely let anything interfere with this plan, even though well-meaning friends and relatives will sometimes make it difficult.

Do not have any sugar, mayonnaise, margarine or other refined foods in the house.

Exclude all so-called foods that are high in calories with minimal or no nutrition.

Eat whole grain products (bread or cereal) at every meal because they are low in calories but high in fiber and food value.

It will take only a few minutes to count the fresh vegetables in your market. In January, I found 55 different ones. There were 21 fresh fruits even in midwinter.

There are about 12 grains and an equal number of legumes plus seeds and nuts so your food program has fantastic possibilities.

Here are the 3 rules that can help you attain an ideal weight.
1) Eat food as close to the way it grows as possible.
2) Have a wide variety over a week's time.
3) Eat enough food to maintain your correct weight
   at your exercise level.

Keep your salt intake low, so start with ½ the amount a recipe calls for. Use fresh lemon juice and learn to use herbs for seasoning. Use small amounts of herbs until you decide on the ones you and your family like and how much.

The ten worst junk foods should never waste your money. They are:

1) All soft drinks

2) White flour products

3) Sweet rolls and pastry

4) Candy

5) Fruit drinks

6) Heavily salted snacks

7) Fats such as cooking oils, mayonnaise, margarine, shortenings, butter, salad dressings and cheese.

8) Potato chips (a baked potato is an excellent food, about 80–90 calories). One potato made into French fries is 274 calories and one potato made into chips is 565 calories and has almost no nutrients.

9) Frozen desserts, some of which have no food at all but are just chemicals.

10) Imitation foods such as dairy substitutes and instant meals.

The average American eats over 100 pounds of refined sugar a year but sugar addicts will never admit it, any more than an alcoholic will admit he drinks too much. A recovering alcoholic can never have even one drink. An ex-smoker cannot have one cigarette and fatties or ex-fatties should not have any refined sugars, chocolate, or visible (free) fats. Honey is at least 80% sugar, by the way.

This section has menus-suggestions-meanings.

1) Main meals should be in the morning or at noon, if at all possible.

2) We have had our vegetables, entree, and salad at 7 a.m. for many years. Our five children grew up this way and still follow the plan or at least have a generous morning meal.

3) When you combine a grain and legume, you have the essential amino acids or protein. It is easier to get too much protein than too little, since nearly all natural food has some protein.

4) Vegetable relishes are raw vegetables such as carrot and celery sticks, cauliflower, green peppers, radishes, onions, zucchini, cucumbers, turnips, kohlrabi, etc. You can use these vegetables, in season, every day, if you wish, since they are low in calories, filling, and high in nutrients.

5) Have a variety of foods over a week's time.

6) The largest meal should include vegetables (raw and cooked), a main dish, and whole grain bread.

7) The breakfast meal should have 2 or 3 fruits (separate or combined), whole grain cereal, and/or bread.

8) The third meal can be fruit and bread or vegetable soup or salad and bread.

9) All breads and cereals should be whole grain and a combination of grains is better than just wheat.

10) Chewy food takes longer to eat, so gives your appetite a chance to work.

11) Cook vegetables a short time and steaming is the best method. Do not peel potatoes and carrots.

12) Have different kinds of bread for taste and health.

13) Vary grains, legumes, and nuts.

14) Do not settle for 3 or 4 vegetables and fruits. Use many varieties, so you do not feel limited.

BREAD
(Dough Hook Method)

Put in the bowl:

5 c hot water

**⅓ c. peanut oil or
   1 avocado**

1 c apple or pear sauce

2 T. salt

1 c. do-pep or soy flour

3 T. dry yeast

Add about 16 cups whole grain flour. Beat 10 minutes. Put in pans and let rise until double in size. Bake at 350° until done.

BREAD
(Regular Method)

Put in largest electric mixer bowl:

5 c. hot water

**⅓ c. peanut oil or
   1 avocado**

1 c. apple or pear sauce

2 T. salt

1 c. do-pep or soy flour

3 T. dry yeast

10 c. whole grain flour

Mix these ingredients at least 10 minutes. Add enough more flour to kneading consistency and knead 10 minutes. Let dough rise until double in size. Punch down and form into loaves. Let rise until double in size and bake at 350° until done.

All of the recipes for the following menus are in this cookbook.

Vegetable Meal Menus

Fruit Meal Menus

Serve whole-grain bread with each meal. In season fresh fruit should be used also.

Third Meal Menus

Vegetable soups or salads or fruits plus bread. You can use any salads in the book or have 2 or 3 fruits with bread and/or cereal.

Following are a list of soups:

Sack Lunches

Fruits

You are not limited to oranges, apples or bananas. Try grapes, melons, fruits canned in juice, grapefruit slices, berries, etc. Score citrus fruits for easy peeling.

Raw Vegetables

Not only carrots and celery but radishes, kholrabi, zucchini, turnips, green peppers, cauliflower, cherry tomatoes, broccoli or cucumbers.

Sandwiches

Use a variety of whole grain bread, rolls, and crackers.

Fillings

Use peanut butter with sugarless jams or raisins or banana slices. There are numerous patties or vegetarian burgers or mash any legume (beans). Add sprouts and/or tomatoes, onions, avocados, diced celery, spinach leaves.

Cereals

Combine home-made granola or brown rice, barley, oat groats with fruits such as applesauce or any blended fruit canned in juice or berries canned or frozen without sugar or dried fruit soaked overnight in juice.

Cookies

Very Special Treats

Time and Money Savers

1) Preserve or freeze but always use leftovers.

   Vegetables, legumes, and grains become soups, stews, salads or casseroles.

   Fruits become desserts or salads or cereal toppings.

2) Plan your grocery list and stick to it. In fact, stay away from the aisles of junk in your supermarket.

3) A garden, orchard, picking your own produce and joining in cooperative buying all cut costs.

4) Sometimes fruits and vegetables are available at little or no cost, just for the gathering.

5) Learn to make your own bread, granola, nut butter, fruit jams, etc.

6) Buy in bulk quantities.

7) Avoid costly high-calorie low-nutrition foods.

8) Good food, water to drink, free fresh air and sunshine also mean less doctor and dental bills.

9) When you are cooking legumes or grains cook enough for several meals. They freeze well and are ready quickly, when you need them.

10) Cook for several meals at one time or cook a future meal while you are eating one. This saves time, fuel, and energy.

11) Use in season produce, can fruits in juices, freeze available vegetables and dry fruits and vegetables.

12) Leave out high cost ingredients whenever feasible.

13) Menus for a week or a month help you to plan for necessary ingredients. This saves gas and time running to the store for one or two items.

14) Make a quantity of food on high energy, less busy days for rushed or lazy days.

15) Fill your oven when you have it heated.

16) Appliances that shut off automatically use less electricity.

17) Top of the stove cooking uses the most fuel, so learn when to turn off the burners. The food continues to cook 5 to 30 minutes.

Exercise

One author has told us that more disease is caused by laziness than poor food.

Exercise is vital to good health and an essential to correct weight.

Exercise increases the efficiency of the lungs, heart and blood vessels. Exercise slows the aging process and helps you look and feel better.

Walking is the best exercise and nearly everyone can do it.

Exercise increases metabolism-that magic item that dissolves fat. For weight control walk a minimum of 45 to 60 minutes every day. Walk slowly enough to carry on a conversation. The length of time is more important than distance or speed.

Please do not say you do not have time to walk, because it is not true. All of us have time for essentials and the same 24 hours a day.

Exercise is for everyone.

Walking outdoors also gives us fresh air and sunshine.

Your exercise should be suitable for your age and physical abilities.

I started walking one-half block with a cane for support. I now walk 3 miles in an hour and I love it. Outdoor exercise is best, but at least open the windows.

Dress warmly in garments that stretch for walking and calisthenics. Be certain your shoes give excellent support and though they are fairly expensive, the shoes last for years.

Do calisthenics exercises suitable for you. Do them slowly because they are then much more effective. Stretch or bend and then relax is a good rule. Use a firm surface, such as grassy ground or a carpeted floor, not a bed, for calisthenics.

Start your exercise program at 10 minutes and gradually work up to 30 minutes daily.

Enjoy!   **Enjoy!**   **Enjoy!**

Here is a Home Exercise Program given to me at a Pain Control Center:

I   Position: Backlying, knees flexed, feet flat on the floor.

1. PELVIC TILT: Flatten low back. Hold for a count of 3. Release. Maintain pelvic tilt in all of the following exercises:

2. PARTIAL SIT UP: Chin to chest, raise head, reach hands to top of knees. Lower hands, lower head, release chin.

3. ELBOWS TO KNEE: Place hands on shoulders. Take elbow to opposite knee. This may be done with the head on the floor initially. Progress to raising head.

4. STRAIGHT LEG RAISE: Flex the opposite knee. Tighten the thigh muscles of the straight leg. Raise leg slowly and lower slowly. Maintain pelvic tilt throughout.

5. HIP AND KNEE ROLL: Press knees together. Roll knees to one side, raise up to mid-line, roll to the opposite side. Maintain pelvic tilt throughout.

6. 8-COUNT ARM EXERCISE: 1—up, 2—above head, 3—up, 4—out to side, 5—up, 6—touch opposite shoulders, 7—up, 8—arms to side.

II   Position: Sidelying.

1. STRAIGHT LEG RAISING: Be sure that leg is in line with trunk, the underneath knee is flexed.

III   Position: Long-sitting, leaning up against a wall, progress to free sitting.

1. QUADRICEPS SET: Tighten thigh muscles, press knees down into floor, pull toes up towards the ceiling. Hold strongly for a count of 5, release. Repeat with the opposite leg.

2. HAMSTRING STRETCH: One knee flexed one knee straight. Hold flexed knee with one hand. Reach the other hand towards the toes of the straight leg, hold for a count of 5, release. Repeat with the opposite leg.

3. TRUNK FORWARD FLEXION: Separate feet as wide apart as is comfortable, rotate feet outwards. Place hands on the insides of the knees. Flex elbows to bring trunk forwards. Back should be straight throughout movement. Progress to free sitting (away from wall) reaching hands towards toes.

IV Position: Hands and knees, hands placed directly beneath shoulders. Maintain a right angle at all joints.

1. MADCAT: Arch low back in to pelvic tilt position, pulling in with the abdominal muscles, tuck buttocks under so back is rounded. Reverse movement until back is flat.

2. ROCKING: Pelvic tilt, round low back, sit back on heels, keep head low. Maintain straight arms throughout. Return to starting position.

3. REACHING AROUND FROM SIDE TO SIDE: Touch foot with hand of same side, turn head to look at foot. Repeat to opposite side.

4. TRUNK TWIST: Reach hand under arch to touch opposite shoulder, bring hand out and straighten outwards and upwards to the same side. Turn head to watch hand throughout movement. Repeat opposite side.

V Position: Sitting on the front half of a straight back chair.

1. FORWARD BENDING: With knees apart, curl trunk forward as you breathe out, arms should be relaxed and forwards. Raise trunk as you breathe in.

2. GLIDING: Keeping arms out to the side and in line with the trunk, bend slowly from side to side.

3. SHOULDER ROLLING: Circle shoulders a) forwards b) backwards.

4. NECK MOVEMENTS: Maintain upright posture of head and shoulders throughout.
   i) forwards and backwards
   ii) side to side
   iii) ear to shoulder

VI Position: Standing

1. PELVIC TILT: Lean back against a wall. Place the heel of one foot against the wall also, place the other foot in front in a normal walking pace position.

   Slide back down wall until the low back is in contact with the wall. The knees will have to be flexed to maintain this position. Hold pelvic tilt. Take one step away from the wall, return back to the wall to see if you have maintained the pelvic tilt.

2. SIDE STRETCH: Stand alongside wall with feet together, extend arm out sideways to touch wall. Lean inwards towards wall.

3. ARM CIRCLES: Stand with arms out sideways. Rotate arms in widening circles a) forwards b) backwards.

VII Position: Walking.

1. TOE WALK

2. HEEL WALK

3. STEP-SQUAT-STAND:

a. Take normal size step

b. Flex knees

c. Straighten knees

Progress by flexing knees more during part b of the exercise.

Water

Life itself depends on water and over one-half of your own body is water.

You lose about 2 to 2½ quarts of water each day and for good health you must take in at least this much through food eaten and water drunk.

Thirst is not always a reliable guide to your need for water, so drink even if you are not thirsty. An adult needs 8 to 10 glasses of water per day.

If you need to learn to drink enough, fill a 2 quart pitcher full of water in the morning. Drink from this pitcher and it should be empty at the end of the day.

Drinking a lot of water increases your endurance to resist disease and promotes better circulation of your lifeblood.

Do not drink with meals, as it delays digestion. Water is the only drink you ever need.

Use water freely on the outside also. A daily bath or shower is essential to remove body wastes.

Relaxing by a stream, lake, or the ocean promotes health.

Thank God for the marvelous life-giving, health-promoting gift of water.

An abundance is a necessity for weight control and drink it between meals. Drink at least ½ hour before meals and 1 hour after eating.

Sunshine

"One of the most healing agents of nature is sunshine," comments one author.

Through its abuse, however, 220,000 persons every year in the United States discover they have skin cancer. Five thousand of these Americans die each year, as a result of too much solar radiation.

The proper amount of sun gives you Vitamin D, kills harmful bacteria and virus, lowers cholesterol and triglyceride levels, increases liver function and promotes healing of wounds.

That lovely sunshine also helps your heart, lungs, and blood vessels to do their work efficiently.

Sunshine lowers blood pressure, helps you resist disease, and it aids your metabolism in burning up fat cells quickly.

Get outdoors regardless of the weather, because you get the benefit of ultraviolet rays, even on a rainy or snowy day.

When at all possible, sunbathe outdoors before 10 a.m. or after 3 p.m. in the Snowbelt and before 9 a.m. or after 4 p.m. in the Sunbelt. There are fluorescent sunlamps available for indoor sunbathing but they are second best and use them with the utmost caution.

It has been learned through research that a person on a low fat diet can take more sun rays without burning.

Let us be grateful for and take advantage of God's life-giving, health producing power that He has given us in sunlight.

Temperance

I am enclosing here some quotations from an author who wrote hundreds of pages on temperance and also lectured widely on this subject. I am in agreement with the statements and know these principles will help you in reaching and maintaining your ideal weight.

"In order to preserve health, temperance in all things is necessary temperance in labor, temperance in eating and drinking."[1]

"The only safe course is to touch not, taste not, handle not, tea, coffee, wines, tobacco, opium, and alcoholic drinks,"[2]

"Temperance reformers have a work to do in educating the people in these lines. Teach them that health, character, and even life, are endangered by the use of stimulants, which excite the exhausted energies to unnatural, spasmodic action."

"Indulgence of appetite is the greatest cause of physical and mental debility, and lies at the foundation of the feebleness which is apparent everywhere."[4]

"When the appetite for spirituous liquor is indulged...reason is paralyzed."[5]

"Tobacco, in whatever form it is used, tells upon the constitution. It is a slow poison. It affects the brain and benumbs the sensibilities..."[6]

"Those who engaged in running the race to obtain that laurel which was considered a special honor, were temperate in all things, so that their muscles, their brains, and every part of them, might be in the very best condition to run."[7]

"It is a great thing to insure health by placing ourselves in right relations to the laws of life."[8]

"The harmonious, healthy action of all the powers of body and mind results in happiness; the more elevated and refined the powers, the more pure and unalloyed the happiness."[9]

"Far too much sugar is ordinarily used in food. Cakes, sweet puddings, pastries, jellies, jams, are active causes of indigestion."[10]

"The less that condiments and desserts are placed upon our tables, the better it will be for all who partake of the food."[11]

"The free use of sugar in any form tends to clog the system, and is not infrequently a cause of disease."[12]

"All should be acquainted with the special value of fruits and vegetables fresh from the orchard and garden."[13]

"Show a purity of taste, appetite, and habits that bears comparison with Daniel's. God will reward you with calm nerves, a clear brain, and unimpaired judgment, keen perceptions."[14]

Temperance enters into every area of our lives. The dictionary defines it as moderation—a desired virtue—and as self control and calmness.

Total abstinence is essential in most areas because of the addiction.

Most of us want clear minds and healthy bodies, so let us rid ourselves of harmful chemicals in food and drink and drugs.

1. CDF 23, 2. CDF 428, 3. CDF 429–430, 4. Te 15, 5. Te 23, 6.Te 55, 7. CH 46–47, 8. CH 499, CH 51, 10. CDF 113, 11. CDF 113, 12. CDF 197, 13. CDF 321, 14. MYP 224 (Complete Titles listed on pg. 33)

Air

A free abundance of fresh air is a blessing available to all.

Many die because they deny themselves fresh air to keep their health or restore diseased bodies.

Sick people especially need fresh air at all times.

Let fresh air into your homes daily and keep windows open at night regardless of the weather.

One author writes:

"In order to have good blood, we must breathe well. Full, deep inspirations of pure air which fill the lungs with oxygen, purify the blood. They impart to it a bright color, and send it, a life-giving current, to every part of the body. A good respiration soothes the nerves-, it stimulates the appetite, and renders digestion more perfect; and it induces sound, refreshing sleep,"[1]

"Air, air, the precious boon of heaven, which all may have, will bless you with its invigorating influence, if you will not refuse it entrance. Welcome it, cultivate a love for it, and it will prove a precious soother of the nerves. Air must be in constant circulation to be kept pure. The influence of pure fresh air is to cause the blood to circulate healthfully through the system. It refreshes the body, and fends to render it strong and healthy, while at the same time its influence is decidedly felt upon the mind, imparting a degree of composure and serenity. It excites the appetite, and renders the digestion of food more perfect, and induces sound and sweet sleep."[2]

"Life in the open air is good for body and mind. It is God's medicine for the restoration of health. Pure air, good water, sunshine, the beautiful surroundings of nature-these are His means for restoring the sick to health in natural ways. To the sick it is worth more than silver or gold to lie in the sunshine or in the shade of the trees."[3]

Deep breathing helps you to relax and can help you to go to sleep.

Fresh air is vital to good health and activates your metabolism. Slim bodies are more likely to be healthy ones.

1. CH 59, 2. CH 60, 3. CH 166 (Complete Titles listed on pg. 33)

Rest

The human body and mind must have rest and a change of pace to function properly.

A regular time to go to bed and a regular time to get up should be followed every day of the week. It is vital to good health and has a definite effect on weight control.

The amount of sleep needed is not the same for each person but regularity is for everyone.

While we sleep our minds and bodies are going through a restorative process, which they need.

People deprived of rest can become both physically and mentally ill.

Never eat later then 4 hours before retiring.

Deep breathing and light exercise just before bedtime promotes relaxation to help you get to sleep and a lukewarm soak in a tub may help also.

Learn techniques to relax your body and mind completely.

People who engage in mostly "sit-down" jobs need physical exercise for a change and to maintain health,

Recreation should be just that-time and activity which will recreate mental, physical, and spiritual processes.

One author has made this suggestion:

"Let several families living in a city or village unite and leave the occupations which have taxed them physically and mentally, and make an excursion into the country, to the side of a fine lake, or to a nice grove, where the scenery of nature is beautiful. They should provide themselves with plain, hygienic food, the very best fruits and grains, and spread their table under the shade of some tree, or under the canopy of heaven. The ride, the exercise, and the scenery, will quicken the appetite, and they can enjoy a repast which kings might envy.

"On such occasions parents and children should feel free from care, labor, and perplexity. Parents should become children with their children, making everything as pleasant for them as possible. Let the whole day be given to recreation. Exercise in the open air, for those whose employment has been within doors and sedentary, will be beneficial to health. All who can, should feel it a duty to pursue this course. Nothing will be lost, but much gained. They can return to their occupations with new life and new courage to engage in their labor with zeal, and they are better prepared to resist disease." [1]

Happy Dreams!

1. CH 195–196 (Complete Titles listed on pg. 33)

Trust

Belief in your God-given abilities will be a tremendous aid in reaching and maintaining your goal of maximum health.

Learn to relax completely. It will take time but it is well worth the effort to learn to relax physically and mentally.

The best method I have found is to concentrate on one area, such as the left hand, until it is totally limp and then move on, until your entire body is void of all tension.

Twenty-five things that will help you to have a peaceful, productive life are:

1) Get plenty of exercise

2) Get enough rest for your needs.

3) Eat regular, natural food meals always-no sugar.

4) Do the things you know are right and good.

5) Find an outlet for your creative abilities in a hobby or recreation.

6) Do something nice for someone often.

7) Stop to smell the roses, listen to a child, and touch the elderly.

8) Smile-smile-smile.

9) Listen-really listen-for the ticking of a clock, bird songs, falling rain, or your own breathing.

10) Plan some idle time every day.

11) Read something that requires concentration.

12) Have a place to be alone.

13) Avoid people who irritate you, whenever possible.

14) Plan vacations for leisure.

15) Do something to give yourself a better life.

16) Live by months and years instead of minutes and seconds.

17) Concentrate on one objective at a time.

18) Keep happy thoughts.

19) Let a clear conscience be your tranquilizer.

20) Be gracious about others shortcomings but critical of your own.

21) Take deep breaths of fresh air several times a day.

22) Have adequate clothing and bedding, so your entire body is warm day and night, indoors and outdoors.

23) Take a daily bath or shower.

24) Drink 8–10 glasses of water daily.

25) Pray.

Summary

Here are some helpers on the way to the correct size you. The results are guaranteed.

1) Get adequate rest.

2) Exercise daily.

3) Get plenty of fresh air and sunshine.

4) Make eating and food preparation a secondary part of your life.

5) Be sure your food looks good, tastes good, and is good nutritionally.

6) Set a good example and a silent one, unless you are asked for help.

7) Eat regularly so you do not get hungry.

8) Eat happily.

9) Put all of the food to be eaten at the meal on your plate at one time.

10) No second helpings.

11) Take smaller portions of the higher calorie foods.

12) Limit even nutritious desserts to once or twice a week.

13) Eat slowly.

14) Learn to say, "No, thank you," sweetly, and mean it.

15) Weigh only once *a week* and your goal is one pound each week. Never have a goal of 5 pounds or 25 pounds or 50 pounds over any length of time. Your goal is one pound in seven days and no panic if you don't lose it.

16) Many will find help in a prayer before each meal asking for wisdom and self control.

17) Breakfast like a king, lunch like a queen, and eat a pauper's supper.

18) Have your three meals 5 to 5½ hours apart.

19) A graph for 6 to 12 months, on which to chart your progress will help you!

20) Many are benefited by group therapy, so join up with your friends who need a weight change also.

21) Never never never eat between meals.

22) Drink plain water only and lots of it between meals.

23) No coffee, tea, alcohol, or soft drinks ever.

24) Make menus for at least one week and preferably for one month. In this book there are 35 days of menus.

25) Eat abundantly of fruits and vegetables prepared simply but tastefully.

26) Use whole grains every meal.

"Pure air, sunlight, abstemiousness, rest, exercise, proper diet, the use of water, trust in divine power-these are the true remedies. Every person should have a knowledge of nature's remedial agencies and how to apply them."[1]

"So closely is health related to our happiness, that we cannot have the latter without the former. A practical knowledge of the science of human life is necessary in order to glorify God in our bodies. It is therefore of the highest importance, that among the studies selected for childhood, physiology should occupy the first place. How few know anything about the structure and functions of their own bodies, and of nature's laws! Many are drifting about without compass or anchor; and what is more, they are not interested to learn how to keep their bodies in a healthy condition, and prevent disease."[2]

"Another precious blessing is proper exercise. There are many indolent, inactive ones who are disinclined to physical labor or exercise because it wearies them. Why does it weary them? The reason why they become weary is that they do not strengthen their muscles by exercise, therefore they feel the least exertion."[3]

"When the weather will permit, all who can possibly do so ought to walk in the open air every day, summer and winter."[4]

"Those who are always busy, and go cheerfully about the performance of their daily tasks, are the most happy and healthy."[5]

Remember that Jesus tells us in III John, verse 2:

"Dear Friend, I pray that you may enjoy good health and that all may go well with you." NIV

I, Lorine Tadej, desire you to have healthy happiness.

Put the following list where you will read it at the beginning of every day. It may help your "I Choose Power."

"Just for Today"

1) Just for today I will eat 2 or 3 fresh fruits.
2) Just for today I will eat some green and yellow vegetables.
3) Just for today I will eat whole-grain cereals and bread.
4) Just for today I will eat legumes (beans) and no meat.
5) Just for today I will take a long leisurely walk.
6) Just for today I will be thankful-whatever the weather.
7) Just for today I will drink 8 glasses of water.
8) Just for today I will spend 8 relaxed hours in bed.
9) Just for today I will get fresh air day and night.
10) Just for today I will express gratitude to God for at least ten things.

1. CH 90, 2. CH 38, 3. CH 52, 4. CH 52, CH 53. Books quoted are by Ellen G. White and include: CDF Counsels on Diet & Foods, CH Counsels on Health, MH Ministry of Healing, MYP Messages to Young People, TE Temperance

Testimonial Letters

Here are six experiences from friends who have adopted this lifestyle.

Dear Friends,

I'm the type who always gains weight even if I only breathe the food I'm around.

I've tried every so-called organic diet method I could get my hands on. I would not take any drugs.

Then I heard more and more about this diet of eating all foods in the unrefined state, no oils and no sugars. I bought these foods and stocked our cupboards.

Shortly after this my husband was diagnosed as diabetic.

To my surprise, our doctor recommended this very diet as the best diet for a diabetic.

We both went on the diet and my husband's blood sugar dropped and I lost 30 pounds.

I ate 3 meals a day and felt so good.

As time slipped by, I've slipped now and then, but always feel that old oppressed feeling I'd had in the past come back on me.

I feel better all the time, so the better I feel the worse I feel when I slip off the diet.

I feet my diet is like my relationship with Christ. If I slip and fall, and I do, I just reach out and get right back on track. The price is too high to allow myself to stay off of it.

Sincerely in Christ,
Shirley Hare

Dear Friends,

I would like to write this letter to you to tell you how a proper diet has changed my life.

My former meals consisted of whatever was to my liking. I loved meat, a good cup of coffee and white bread with lots of butter on it. I did not care for vegetables.

I began to have trouble with my stomach and after going from doctor to doctor and taking hundreds of pills, I finally ended up in the hospital, where I had a major operation for diverticulitis. After recovering from the operation I was sent home. I still had digestive problems, so I returned to the hospital where the doctors discovered I also had ulcerated colitis. For this I had to take treatments for months.

Fortunately, I found someone who could tell me what had caused my problems and what to do to overcome such conditions as diverticulitis and colitis. It was all in the food that I had been eating.

My diet was changed to WHOLE WHEAT BREAD, GRAINS, VEGETABLES and such things as the Good Lord had intended for our diet in the first place. No coffee, tea or oils, and the best part is that you learn to enjoy and like this type of a diet.

April 1982 I was 78 years old and am feeling fine. I am able to do several hours of yard work daily. If only I had started this diet or I should say type of eating when I was fifty years or younger, I would have saved myself many dollars and a lot of suffering,

I would like to recommend this method of foods to everyone, and would suggest that they don't wait until they are sick but start when they are young and healthy.

Sincerely,
Ernest C. Comer

Dear Friends,

When I went on this lifestyle which included exercise in the fresh air, sunshine, only sugar as found in natural foods like dates, raisins, etc., no free fats and trust in my Heavenly Father. I lost 20 pounds immediately and then gained gradually back until I now weigh the recommended weight for my height and frame which is easily held at this level. My blood pressure came down to 127/78. I feel good, enjoy good health, praise God, I give Him all the praise.

Allen Field

Dear Friends,

I will soon be seventy-one years old. I weighed two hundred pounds by the age of nine. I had headaches often all my life. At thirty-six years I weighed 285 lbs. I had problems if I ate much raw food of any kind.

I would be running to the toilet several times at night plus several times during the day.

Then about five years ago I started having ulcers on my feet. It would take weeks to get them healed up and then before long they would come again.

Finally, last September I lost my right leg because of hardening of the arteries. When I came home from the hospital eight months ago I started eating the way God intended us to eat in the beginning.

We eat no refined food, no sugar, no free fats, no concentrated proteins, very little salt.

I seldom have headaches any more. I eat lots of raw fruits and vegetables with no bowel problems. I weigh 160 lbs. and eat all I want without gaining.

I haven't had any ulcers on my left foot for eight whole months. I thank the Lord for what He has done for me. He keeps His promises when we honor Him by obeying His word.

Herbert Young

"Always Over Weight"

Dear Friends,

All my life I've had to fight a weight problem. I've tried every diet that I ever heard about. Sometimes I would lose a few pounds—but I always gained it back, and more too. I always had to buy ugly clothes, mu mu type and such. I was always the biggest one in my family.

When my mother was put in a nursing home close to where I live I would spend three to four days a week with her. There was a ramp I had to climb three floors up. I started losing weight so I decided to take advantage of it. I put myself on a diet of my own. I gave up oils of every kind and all sugar and salt.

I exercised every morning for about 20 minutes and I rode my exercise bike for 5 miles each morning. I am up to 10 miles a day now.

Now I am the thinnest one in my family and I am very happy. I have a heart problem which is very much improved. I can buy nice clothes, no more mu mus.

I think most important is that I asked God's help and He answered my prayer.

I have lost 65 pounds.

Thank you Jesus,

Marjorie Starr

Mildred Haubry told her story to me, Lorine Tadej, and I want to share some of her experiences with you.

Mildred has been a non-meat eater for 30 years but a totally natural foods eater only a little over a year at this writing.

She had been a diabetic for nineteen years and on 50 units of insulin daily for ten years.

Mildred had been very ill and extremely depressed for 13 years, during which time she took tranquilizers continuously. The drugs, depression and other illnesses turned her into a recluse.

Five years ago Mildred was nearly blind, as a result of the diabetes.

About 15 months ago, Mildred Haubry listened to a series of taped messages by [the late] Dr. Zane Kime. He recommended God's lifestyle in using unrefined foods, no sugar, no free fats, whole grains, legumes, vegetables and fruits, daily exercise suitable to age and ability, sunlight, fresh air, at least 6 to 8 glasses of water for God's healing through His laws of health and happiness.

Mildred had only one direction to move, since she had hit bottom health wise.

She is now a delightful, vivacious lady.

She has taken no insulin and no tranquilizers for many months.

She has lost 60 excess pounds without effort and her eyesight has remarkably improved. Her doctor says it is almost unbelievable.

Mildred knows that God answers prayer and gives physical, mental and spiritual health.

Recipe Section

If you do not want to use mushrooms, they are optional in most recipes.

I use Pam as a spray on pans that do not have a non-stick surface, since it contains lecithin, is convenient to use, and is low calorie.

Cinnamon is a slightly irritating spice. If it bothers your stomach, you can use coriander or cardamom instead or combine them.

Soy sauce is a fermented substance, but two items that take the place of soy sauce in all recipes are Dr. Bronner's Balanced Soya-Mineral Bullion or Bragg's Liquid Aminos. Both of these are usually found in health food stores or cooperative stores.

We do want our food to taste good, so our families will eat it. Be sure to ask God to help you to enjoy His program for a healthful lifestyle.

Our protein should be not more than 10% of our caloric intake. Research has shown that all Americans get more protein than needed and too much of it can lower resistance to disease, increase the aging process, decrease assimilation of needed nutrients and cause much loss of calcium which leads to osteoporosis.

You should have unprocessed proteins for breakfast, when you should eat ⅓ to ½ of your daily needed nutrients.

If lunch contains natural protein foods, the evening meal does not need them.

Please remember that fruit and vegetables should always make up the largest part of a meal.

SALT SUBSTITUTE

2 t garlic powder	1 t lemon rind, powdered
1 t basil	1 t oregano
1 t anise seed, finely ground	

Mix together and store in tightly closed container.

Use one of the 3 following Chicken-Style Seasoning recipes or McKay's Chicken-Style Seasoning without MSG (Monosodium Glutamate).

CHICKEN-STYLE SEASONING I

1/3 c food yeast, flaked	1 t onion powder
3/4 t bell pepper, dry	1/2 t sage
3/4 t salt (opt)	1/2 t thyme
1/2 t celery salt	1/4 t marjoram
1/2 t garlic powder	1 T parsley flakes

Grind all ingredients together and store in a tightly covered container.

CHICKEN-STYLE SEASONING II

2 T celery salt	2 T onion powder
2 T parsley flakes	2 T turmeric
1/4 c salt	1/2 t garlic powder
1/4 t marjoram	1/4 t savory

Mix ingredients well and store in tightly sealed jar.

CHICKEN-STYLE SEASONING III

1 1/3 c brewer's yeast	2 T turmeric
2 t garlic powder	1/2 t garlic powder
1/4 c salt	1/4 t parsley flakes
1 T onion powder	

Mix all ingredients together. Store in a tightly sealed jar.

BURGER RELISH

1/3 c cucumber, shredded	1/4 c parsley, minced
1/4 c radishes, shredded	3 T Soyannaise
2 T onion, grated	1/2 t garlic salt
1/4 c celery, minced	1 T lemon juice

Drain first 3 ingredients well. Combine all ingredients; mix well. Cover and store in refrigerator.

The preceding recipes are from Adams Table Cookbook, used by permission.

Breads

Non-Yeast Breads:

ALMOND PIE CRUST

1½ c ground almonds   2 t water
3 T flour   ¼ t salt

Grind nuts in grinder. Mix flour, nut meal and salt, add water and mix well. Press into pie pan. Bake at 300° for 45 minutes. Use with pie filling.

BOSTON BROWN BREAD

4 c whole grain flours   1 c chopped nuts
⅓ c molasses   1 T grated orange rind
1 c raisins   1 t salt
2 c water

Mix; put in a Pam sprayed Pyrex or stainless steel mixing bowl. Steam for 2 hours in a covered kettle.

CASHEW CRACKERS

Blend:

1 c raw cashews   ½ c hot water
½ t salt

Add:

1 c whole wheat flour

Spread thin on a cookie sheet. Bake at 350° until crisp, at least 30 minutes.

CORN CRACKERS

2 c cornmeal   1 t salt
1 c cashew meal (blended)   4 T sesame seed
1 c walnut meal (blended)   1 c water

Spread very thin on a cookie sheet. Bake at 250° until very dry.

CORN MUFFINS

Blend:

2 c soaked soybeans, well drained

8 dates

2 t salt

2 c hot water

¼ c raw oatmeal

Add:

2 c cornmeal

Fill muffin tins and bake at 400° for 35 minutes.

CORNMEAL RICE CAKES

1 c cornmeal

4 Tbsp soy flour

½ tsp salt

1 c cooked rice

½ c ground sunflower seeds

1 c boiling water

Mix cornmeal, flour and salt. Add boiling water. Mix well until moisture is absorbed. Add rice and sunflower seeds. Mix. Place in mounds on cookie sheet, flatten to about ½ inch thickness. Bake at 400° for 30 minutes, or until brown.

FRENCH TOAST

Blend and then pour into a shallow dish:

1 c hot water

1 c apple juice

1 c raw cashews

6 dates

½ t salt

¼ c whole wheat flour

Dip bread slices in the batter and brown slowly on both sides in a non stick or Pam-sprayed pan. Top with any fruit or berries hot or cold.

GRANOLA

Mix:

3 c rolled oats

1 c whole wheat flour

½ c cornmeal

½ c rye flour

½ c millet meal

½ c wheat germ

½ c coconut

½ c sunflower seeds

½ c sesame seeds

Blend and add, then mix well:

1 c peanut butter

6 oz apple juice conc.

8 dates

1 t vanilla

Spread on cookie sheets and bake at 250° until dry.

OATMEAL CRACKERS

2 c nut meal (blended)	1 t salt
1 c cold water	2 c quick oatmeal

Spread very thin on a cookie sheet. Bake at 250° until completely dry and crisp.

SESAME OAT SQUARES

Blend:

1 c raw cashews	1 c dates
1 c hot water	

Add:

1 ½ c sesame seeds	½ t salt
¾ c soy flour	1 t vanilla
1 c whole wheat flour	

Pat thin and bake until golden brown at 325°.

WAFFLES

⅓ c cashews	¾ c whole wheat flour
1 c water	1 t salt
2½ c oats	4–4½ c hot water
¾ c cornmeal	

Blend cashews and 1 cup water first. Then add alternately with the liquefier on, part of hot water (2 to 3 cups) and all the grains and salt. When blended smoothly, pour batter into a large bowl. Add the rest of the water and mix thoroughly.

Spray waffle iron lightly with Pam while it is still cold. Then put on high heat.

Bake waffles in hot waffle iron for 8 to 12 minutes. Even with many batches, you won't have to use any more Pam. Do not peek for at least 8 minutes.

You will find other Gluten Free recipes in the Gluten Free index at the end of the book.

Gluten Free Rice Waffles

Soak overnight:

3 c rice, whole grain   **½ c soy beans**

Whiz 2¼ c water and 1½ c soaked mix. Add:

**¼ c sesame or sunflower   ¾ c rice, cooked
       seeds   ½ c corn meal**

¼ t salt

Bake in waffle iron about 10 min. Yield 9 waffles or more. Freeze and toast.

NOTE: Recipes containing gluten can be made gluten free by replacing the wheat with rice, millet or corn. Use puffed rice to replace wheat bread crumbs. (Corn pasta is also available.)

WHOLE WHEAT CRACKERS

**4 c whole wheat pastry   ½ c peanut butter
       flour   1 t salt**

1 c water

Mix peanut butter and water. Pour into flour. Roll out thin. Bake at 350° for 20 minutes, or until golden brown.

SOY WAFFLES

Soak overnight:

1 c soybeans

Drain well. Blend thoroughly:

2½ c warm water   ½ c sunflower seeds

1½ c rolled oat   ½ t salt

**   soaked soybeans**

Bake 10–15 minutes in a hot waffle iron. These may be made ahead and reheated.

Yeast Breads:

CORNBREAD

Mix and set aside:

2 T yeast

1 c hot water

½ c applesauce

Mix:

4½ c hot water

½ c oil or 2 blended avocados

1½ T salt

4½ c cornmeal

⅔ c soy flour

¾ c gluten flour (omit this ingredient for gluten free recipe)

Add yeast mixture.

Mix all and add 4 to 6 cups whole wheat flour as needed. Knead 10 minutes. Let rise 45 minutes. Punch down. Put in pans and let rise until double in size. Bake at 350° for 45–60 minutes.

CORN CEREAL OR CORN BREAD

Soak 1 c of whole corn for two days, rinsing and changing water at the end of the first day. After 2 days, rinse and grind in food processor. Put in crock pot with four c cold water, add 1 t salt or 1 T Bragg's Liquid Aminos. Cook 5 to 8 hours (depending on the crock pot you use). Can double recipe if desired.

For Corn Bread, soak 1 c soybeans and add to ground soaked corn along with seasoning and bake until firm.

CORN BUTTER

Whiz in blender:

¼ c water, cold

1 T Emes Kosher-Jel

Let set for 5 minutes. Bring to a boil and simmer ten minutes:

1½ c water

½ c corn flour

¾ c corn, frozen or canned

Add to blender:

1 c water, boiling

1½ c mush (from above)

½ c cashews

1 t salt or Bragg's Liquid Aminos

2 t lemon juice

1 t paprika

2–3 T olive oil

Blend and cool.

KOLACHES

Combine:

1½ c flour	1 c hot water
2 T yeast	1 avocado
½ c applesauce	**blended**
1 t salt	

Beat well, Add 1½ to 2 cups more flour. Mix well. Shape bread into about 1½ inch balls and place on cookie sheet. Let rise 15 minutes. Use 2 fingers and make an indentation in each. Put in 1 teaspoon of filling, pressing with spoon slightly. Let rise 15 minutes. Bake at 400° for 15 to 20 minutes.

Fillings:

A. Dried fruits and/or nuts

B. Vegetables, finely chopped

MULTI-GRAIN BREAD

Liquefy:

5 c warm water	**¾ c date**

Add:

4 c whole wheat flour	**2 pkgs. yeast**

Stir and let rise 30 minutes. Add:

4 T cashew meal (blend)	**½ c oatmeal**
1 T salt	**½ c cornmeal**
3 c whole wheat flour	**½ c soy flour**
¾ c gluten flour	**½ c rye flour**
½ c barley flour	

Knead for 10 minutes. Let rise until double. Knead down. Let rise until double again. Form into loaves. Let rise until double. Bake at 425° for 10 minutes, then at 350° for 40 minutes. Remove immediately from pans.

CHANGE OF FLAVOR IDEAS FOR BREAD

A. Use unsweetened fruit juice instead of water or use tomato juice instead of water.

B. Use vega-salt, onion salt, celery salt or garlic salt.

C. Add chopped dried fruit or nuts to batter.

D. Add chives (dried) or dried or fresh parsley or dried onions to the batter.

BREADS WITH FILLINGS

Pat out the dough for one loaf one inch thick and cover with filling. Roll up the dough and place in bread pan with the overlap at the bottom of your pan. This may be cut as rolls also.

FILLINGS

A. Finely ground nuts

B. Ground dried fruit

C. Finely ground orange or lemon peel

D. Combination of herbs such as sage and parsley or dill, sesame, celery or poppy seed; or sprinkle with garlic or onion powder and paprika, or use your imagination.

E. Homemade peanut butter mixed with ground raisins.

F. Sugarless jam

ONE LOAF BREAD

1 c warm water	**1 T yeast**
½ c applesauce	

Mix and let stand 10 minutes, then add:

1 t salt	**2½ c whole wheat flour**

Knead well, adding flour if needed. Put in loaf pan and let rise to double in size. Bake at 350° for 45 to 50 minutes.

SUNNY SOYA BREAD

Put ½ cup lukewarm water in small bowl; sprinkle in:

1 T dry yeast	**¼ c applesauce**

In blender, mix together:

¼ c applesauce	**2 t salt**
1 c cooked yellow squash	**1 c warm water**

Mix until smooth. Pour into a large bowl. Add:

2 c whole wheat flour

Beat well, then add:

¼ c wheat germ	**½ c soy flour**
½ c sunflower seeds	

Mix and add yeast, Stir in enough flour to make a soft bread dough. Knead until elastic. Put in Pam-sprayed bread pans. Let rise until double. Bake for 35 to 40 minutes in a 375° oven.

WHEAT GERM MUFFINS

Mix together:

1¼ c water

½ c applesauce

2 t yeast

½ t salt

½ t vanilla

¾ c raisins or dates

½ t grated orange rind (optional)

1 c wheat germ whole wheat pastry flour as needed

½ c soy flour

Prepare muffin tins with Pam and fill to ⅔ full. Let rise 30 minutes. Preheat oven to 350°. Bake about 20 minutes. Watch carefully as they tend to burn easily. Yield: 10 to 12 muffins.

ZUCCHINI WHEAT BREAD

In a large mixing bowl, combine:

¼ c warm water

1 pkg. yeast

Let stand 5 minutes to soften. Add:

⅔ c warm water

3 T oil or ½ avocado (mashed)

1 c applesauce

Stir together:

1½ c whole wheat flour

1½ c white flour, unbleached

¼ c wheat germ

1 t salt

1 t grated orange rind

2 t ground cardamom

With a spoon, stir about half of this into the yeast mixture; add:

1½ c zucchini, coarsely shredded

¾ c currants or raisins

Stir to blend. Gradually stir in ½ cup unbleached white flour. Turn dough out onto a well floured board and knead 10 minutes, or until smooth and elastic, adding more flour as necessary to prevent sticking. Place dough in an oiled bowl, turning to oil top; cover and let rise in a warm place until doubled, about 1½ hours.

Punch down dough and divide in half. Shape and knead each half into a loaf and place in a loaf pan. Cover, let rise in a warm place about 45 min. until the dough doubles. Bake at 350° for 40–45 minutes, or until tops are dark brown. Turn out onto racks to cool. Makes 2 loaves.

To make Herb Zucchini Wheat Bread: Follow directions above, but OMIT orange rind, cardamom, and currants. Add ½ teaspoon dry basil, ¼ teaspoon thyme leaves, ¼ teaspoon oregano leaves to flour.

Write your extra recipes here:

Foreign-Style Foods

ARABIC POTATO SALAD

6 c potatoes, diced
      & cooked

1 c onion, diced

½ c parsley, chopped

1 t dill seed

1 clove garlic, diced

½ c lemon juice

1½ c pineapple juice

Mix together.

BRAZILIAN RICE

2 garlic cloves,
    minced

4 c water

1 lg onion, chopped

3 T chicken (See pg. 40)
    or beef-style
    seasoning

2 c brown rice, long grain

Cook until rice is done, then add:

3 c tomatoes, chopped

3 c peanuts or cashews,
    chopped

Serve immediately

CEYLONESE RICE

Mix together in a large skillet.,

2 c brown rice, cooked

1½ c carrot strips, thin

1 c chopped onion

1 bunch scallions, cut in 1
    inch lengths

½ c raisins

Cook, stirring frequently, until vegetables just begin to brown, about 5 minutes. Add:

2 c water

10 oz frozen peas

2 t salt

Bring to boiling, separating peas with a fork. Reduce heat; cover and simmer for 5 minutes. Add 1 cup cashew nuts or pecan halves. Toss lightly. Makes 8 to 10 servings.

CUBAN BLACK BEANS

Soak 1 cup black beans in water overnight. Drain. Add 2 cups cold water. Bring to boil, reduce heat. Then add:

1 sm onion, chopped
½ green pepper,
    chopped

1 garlic clove,
    minced
1 t salt

Simmer until done. Serves 5 to 6.

GERMAN SOUP

Combine:

4 T Beef-style McKay's
     seasoning
3 c water
½ c parsley
2 bay leaves, crushed
2 cans tomatoes or 4 c
      tomatoes, fresh
¼ c lemon juice

1 c sauerkraut
2 garlic cloves, minced
¼ t thyme
4 c potatoes, diced
4 c onions, diced
1 c carrots, shredded
2 t celery seed

Simmer for 1 hour.

INDIAN VEGETABLES

In a large skillet, cook until fork tender:

1½ c water
1 c tomato puree
3 potatoes, sliced
2 onions, thinly sliced

1 t salt
1 t cumin
1 t turmeric (more or
    less to taste)

Add:

3 c tomatoes, chopped
1 can green beans, cut

2 c pinto beans, cooked

Heat and serve over rice.

ITALIAN GREENS SAUCE (For Pasta or Grain)

Cook:

2 lg onions, chopped   **¼ c water**
4 garlic cloves, minced

Add:

3 c cashew cream   **3 pkgs. Swiss chard, frozen, thawed, drained and chopped**

Heat and serve.

ITALIAN POLENTA

In a kettle, mix together:

1 c cornmeal, course ground   **1 T chicken-style seasoning (See pg. 40)**
3 c water or tomato juice

Cook until thick and done. Put into a loaf pan while hot. Cool, slice, cover with ground nuts and brown until crisp in broiler.

ITALIAN VEGETABLE SAUCE

Cook for 20 minutes:

**1 lg eggplant, cubed or
   3 c zucchini, cubed**   **3 onions, chopped fine**
          1 c water

Add:

3 garlic cloves   **2 c olives, chopped**
½ c parsley, chopped   **1 t basil**
2 lbs tomatoes, chopped   **salt, as needed**

Simmer until thick. Serve on pasta.

ITALIANO VEGETABLE SOUP

Mix together:

2 qts hot water   **16 oz tomatoes, canned**
1 c onion, finely chopped   **½ c brown rice**
          2 T chicken-style seasoning (See pg. 40)
1 c celery, finely sliced
1 c carrots, finely sliced
1 c cabbage, chopped   **½ t thyme**
1 c potatoes, cubed   **¼ t oregano**
1 bay leaf, crumbled

Simmer for 45 to 60 minutes.

MEXICAN AVOCADO DRESSING

Blend:

  ½ c cashews, raw   **½ med onion**

  1 c water

When smooth, add:

  2 avocados   **2 T lemon juice**

Blend until creamy.

MEXICAN AVOCADO HUEVOS RANCHEROS

Pour 2 tablespoons water into a frying pan over medium heat; add 1 medium-sized onion, chopped; cook until limp. Then stir in:

15 ozs tomato sauce, canned   **1 t. ground cumin**

  1 garlic clove, minced   **1 t oregano leaves**

  3 T green chiles, canned,   **1 bay leaf**
      seeded & chopped

Simmer, uncovered, 1 0 minutes or longer, until slightly thickened. Season to taste with salt. Cool, cover, and chill as long as 24 hours, if made ahead. Remove bay leaf and reheat, uncovered, to simmering before serving. Peel, pit, and halve 2 avocados; coat cut sides with 2 tablespoons lemon juice and arrange, cut side up, in a 9 inch pie pan. Spoon 1 to 2 tablespoons sauce over top. Broil, about 6 inches from heat. Serve each avocado half on a bed of shredded lettuce. Pass remaining sauce to spoon over all. Makes 4 servings.

MEXICAN ENCHILADAS

Thaw frozen tortillas and dip, one at a time, in tomato juice. Place each tortilla on a large plate and spread with refried beans. Place a heaping tablespoon of enchilada sauce across the center of the tortilla. Roll up the filled tortillas and place loosely in a baking dish. Cover all with more enchilada sauce. Bake at 300° for 30 minutes, until hot.

ENCHILADA SAUCE

4 c onions, chopped   **½ T chicken-style**
                           seasoning

1 c mushrooms,   **(See pg. 40)**
    chopped

1 c olives, olives   **1 t oregano**

1 c tomato juice   **12 ozs tomato paste,**
                            canned

½ t garlic salt

                     16 ozs tomato sauce,
                            canned

Simmer 2 hours.

MEXICAN GUACAMOLE

2 lg tomatoes,
      chopped fine
1 med onion, chopped fine
½ t garlic salt

1 t salt
3 lg avocados, finely
      cubed or mashed

Mix together.

MEXICAN BEANS

Soak 1 cup pinto or red beans overnight. Drain. Add and cook until well done:

1 lg onion, chopped
½ t garlic salt

2½ c water
½ tsp. salt

Mash the beans slightly and add:

¼ t oregano
¼ t cumin

¼ t turmeric

Use as you would refried beans.

MEXICAN BEANS WITH CHILES

3 c red beans, cooked
     & mashed
1 onion, minced
  salt, as needed

4 ozs green chilies,
      canned, drained
      & diced
¾ t oregano

Bake until hot and bubbly.

MEXICAN·CORN

1 can corn
1 c olives, sliced

2 c tomatoes
1 t oregano

Combine; heat and serve.

MEXICAN RICE

1 c brown rice
1¼ c. water
1 c tomato sauce
½ t oregano

1 med onion, chopped
¼ t garlic salt
1 t cumin

Combine and cook until done; add salt, as desired. Just before serving, add 1 can of corn.

MEXICAN SALAD DRESSING

2 c tomato juice
⅓ c lemon juice
¼ c onion, dried
¼ c parsley, dried

vegetable seasoning
   salt, if needed
1 T food yeast
   (Brewers yeast)
½ c olives

Blend well.

MEXICAN-STYLE VEGETABLE RICE

Heat 3 tablespoons water in a frying pan over medium heat. Add:

1 lg onion, chopped
  2 cloves garlic, minced

1½ c brown rice, long grain

Cook, stirring, until onion is limp and rice is opaque. Stir in:

½ t salt
3 t chicken-style
    seasoning
    (See pg. 40)

3 c water

Bring to boiling, cover and simmer 20 minutes, or until liquid is absorbed. To the rice, add:

10 ozs peas and carrots
     (frozen), thawed

1½ c tomatoes, peeled,
      seeded, & chopped

Stir just until blended. Cook over low heat, stirring just until vegetables are heated through, about 3 minutes.

MEXICAN TOSTADOS

Warm tortillas in a Teflon pan and keep warm in the oven. Cover with a towel. Place the tortilla on a plate and top with chili beans or pinto beans and a tossed green salad.

Use Mexican Salad Dressing or Avocado Dressing or Guacamole.

ORIENTAL CHINESE RICE

Cook:

1 c onion, chopped

1 c celery, chopped

2 c mushrooms, sliced

1 c water

1 T chicken-style
seasoning
(See pg. 40)

(Add chicken-style seasoning to water; cook vegetables in this seasoned water.) Add:

1 can water chestnuts,
sliced

3 T soy sauce

3 c brown rice, cooked

Simmer 10 minutes.

ORIENTAL DRESSING FOR VEGETABLES

½ c sesame seed paste

3 T lemon juice

2 T soy sauce

10 dates

½ c hot water

Blend.

ORIENTAL SOYBEANS

Soak, cook and drain 1 cup soybeans. Set aside. Cook until tender, but crisp:

1 lg onion, chopped

2 lg carrots, sliced

1 garlic clove,
finely grated

1 c water

Add:

1 can pineapple chunks

2 tomatoes, chopped

1 T chicken-style
seasoning
(See pg. 40)

1 T soy sauce

2 T cornstarch

2 c pineapple juice

Add the soybeans and cook for about 2 minutes. Serve over brown rice.

ORIENTAL SWEET 'N' SAUCY RICE

Combine:

2 c brown rice, cooked

½ c raisins

½ c pineapple juice

1 T lemon juice

½ c almonds, chopped

Can be served hot or cold.

ORIENTAL SWEET-SOUR SAUCE

Heat:

1 qt pineapple juice
8 ozs orange juice
½ c lemon juice

1 t onion salt
2 T soy sauce

Thicken slightly with cornstarch.

ORIENTAL VEGETABLES

To prepare, use a large skillet or several small pans. Cook vegetables briefly in seasoned water [2 tablespoons chicken-style seasoning (See pg. 40) in 1 quart of water].

You can use any combination of these vegetables your family likes:

zucchini, thin slices
celery, thin,
**   diagonally cut**
Chinese pea pods
bamboo shoots
green onions, cut
**   lengthwise or**
**   onion rings**

green pepper strips
tomatoes, quartered
green beans, whole
bean sprouts
water chestnuts
mushrooms,
**   fresh or canned**

Serve the vegetables on brown rice and top generously with the Sweet-Sour Sauce and whole or sliced almonds.

PARISIAN GREEN LIMAS

In separate pans, cook:

1 pkg green limas (lg.)   **1 pkg broccoli spears**

Place hot broccoli in casserole; pour on hot limas and 1 large can mushroom slices. Blend:

1 c cashews, raw
2 c hot water

1 T chicken-style
**   seasoning**
**   (See pg. 40)**

Pour over vegetables. Heat to bubbling in a 350° oven. Serve.

PORTUGUESE RED BEAN SOUP

Cook about 10 to 15 minutes:

1 qt water

**1 c whole wheat
    macaroni**

**1 lg potato, unpeeled,
     chopped**

Add and cook 5 minutes:

**2 sm head cabbage,
     coarsely chopped**

1 qt water

Add and heat:

1 c tomato sauce

1 T onion powder

1 t garlic powder

1 t paprika

4 c red beans, cooked

PORTUGUESE ZUCCHINI

Cook:

1 onion, finely chopped

1 c red beans, soaked

6 ozs tomato paste

2 c water

**1 t Italian-herb
    seasoning**

When the beans are done, add salt if needed and 3 or 4 medium zucchini, sliced in ⅛ inch pieces. Simmer for about 10 minutes, until crisp-tender. Serve.

PUERTO RICAN BEANS AND RICE

1 lg onion, diced

8 ozs tomato sauce, canned

½ t garlic salt

1 t oregano

1 c water

2 c tomato juice

Cook until onions are done. Add:

**4 c navy or pinto beans,
    cooked**

4 c brown rice, cooked

PUNJAB PEA SOUP

Bring to a boil and simmer for 1 hour:

1 med onion, finely chopped	**1 c split peas, dried**
1 t tumeric	**1 garlic clove, minced**
½ t cumin	**1 bay leaf, crumbled**
5 c water	**2 T chicken-style**
2 med carrots, sliced	**seasoning**
1 T celery seed	**(See pg. 40)**
⅛ t rosemary	**⅛ t thyme**

Blend and serve.

SPANISH GAZPACHO (A Cold Soup)

1 c tomato, chopped	**½ t celery seed**
½ c cucumbers, chopped	**2 T lemon juice**
½ c green onion,	**¼ t garlic powder**
finely chopped	**1 zucchini, thinly sliced**
¼ c parsley, snipped	**3 c tomato juice**
1 T soy sauce	

Combine and chill for at least 4 hours.

SUKIYAKI

Cook for 5 minutes:

1 c water	**1 c onions, thinly sliced**

Add and cook for 5 minutes more:

1 pkg French-style green	**1 pkg broccoli spears,**
beans, frozen	**cut lengthwise if**
	large

Add and cook for 2 minutes:

1 can mushrooms (lg), sliced	**2 c tofu cubes**
1 can No. 2½ bean sprouts	

Thicken slightly and serve with soy sauce.

Fruits

ALMOST ALMOND ROCA

1 c walnuts, ground	3 T carob powder
1 c almonds, raw, ground	½ c orange juice
	3 T Minute Tapioca
1 c coconut, ground	1t vanilla ground nuts
1 c dates, ground	for rolling

Grind nuts and dates through coarse blade of food grinder. Place nuts, dates, coconut and carob powder in mixing bowl. Combine in small saucepan, the orange juice and tapioca. Cook and stir over medium heat until tapioca is clear, about 6 to 8 minutes. Add vanilla.

Combine all ingredients and mix thoroughly. (Fingers work best!) Roll small portions between palms of hands into logs, about 1½ inches in length. Roll logs in ground nuts. Chill until firm. Yield: 2 to 3 dozen pieces. Store in refrigerator.

APPLE DATE SQUARES

Mix together:

2½ c oats	½ c coconut
1 c whole wheat flour	½ c chopped nuts

Spread ¾ of this crumb mixture in a 9 x 12 inch pan. Filling:

4 c shredded apples	3 c orange juice
1 c dates, chopped	1 t vanilla

Pour the filling over the crumb mixture in the pan. Top with the rest of the crumb mixture and bake at 350° for 30 minutes.

ARMENIAN CHRISTMAS PORRIDGE

Combine and cook for 45 minutes:

1 c pearl barley	1 qt water

Add and cook 30 minutes more, uncovered:

2 c apricots, chopped, dried	1 qt water
	1t salt
1½ c raisins	½ t ground coriander

Turn off heat, cover, but leave on burner 1 hour. Serve warm with nut milk. (This porridge can be cooled and reheated.)

NUT MILK

½ c raw nuts (cashews, almonds)

1½ c hot water

½ c dates

dash of salt

1 t vanilla

Thoroughly blend together.

BAKED OATMEAL

Combine:

2½ c rolled oats

4 lg apples, sliced

1 c nuts, chopped

1 c raisins or dates

1 t salt

1 t cinnamon or sub.

Add 1 teaspoon vanilla to 3 cups apple juice and pour over oat mixture. Mix thoroughly. Pour into Pam-sprayed pan. Bake for 1 hour at 350°. Serve with nut milk and nuts on top. Can be made the night before and put on time-bake. The aroma is pleasant to awaken to!

BANANA CREAM PUDDING OR PIE

Blend:

1 c cashews, raw

2 c hot water

24 dates

1½ t vanilla

½ t salt

4 T cornstarch

Add 1 cup hot water; cook until thickened. Cool and add 4 sliced bananas.

BANANA NUT COOKIES

Blend:

½ c dates

½ c cashews, raw

¾ c hot water

Add and mix well:

6 bananas, mashed

1½ c nuts, chopped

1½ c whole wheat flour

3 c rolled oats, raw

2 t vanilla

1 t salt

Drop by spoonfuls on a cookie sheet. Bake at 325° until light brown.

BERRY TOPPINGS

Heat and thicken slightly, 16 ounces apple juice concentrate. Add 1 quart berries and serve on waffles, pancakes, toast or cereals.

BREAD OR RICE PUDDING

Blend:

1 c cashews, raw	2 t vanilla
2 c dates	2 t cinnamon
3 c hot water	

Pour over:

4 c brown rice, cooked, or 6 c whole wheat bread cubes mixed with 1½ c raisins	1 c walnuts, chopped

Bake at 350° for 25 minutes.

CAROB CANDY

Melt slowly on low heat:

4 c peanut butter, old-fashioned	4 c carob chips, date-sweetened

Pour this over 4 cups raisins and 2 large cans crisp oriental noodles. Cool in refrigerator. This makes a large quantity, but freezes well.

CAROB FRUIT BARS

Dissolve 1 tablespoon dry yeast in ¼ cup hot water. Add:

1½ c prunes, cut up	1 c whole wheat flour
1 c raisins	3 T carob powder
1 c dates, chopped	1 c nuts, chopped

Spread 1 inch thick in baking pan and let rise 30 minutes. Bake at 325° for 40 minutes.

CAROB PUDDING

Cook 5 minutes:

1 c water	¼–⅓ c carob powder

Cool slightly. Blend until smooth:

1 c hot water	1 c cashews, raw

Add and continue to blend:

1 c hot water	2 c dates

Combine all ingredients and add:

2 T vanilla	¼ c cornstarch

Bring all to a slow boil to thicken, stirring constantly. Cool in a covered dish. Serve topped with sliced bananas or carob syrup.

CAROB SYRUP

Cook 5 minutes:

1 c water   **½ c carob powder**

Cool slightly. Blend:

2 c hot water   **2 c dates**

Combine ingredients. Use as you would chocolate syrup on banana slices or carob pudding.

CAROB SUPER FUDGE

½ c carob powder   **½ c water**

Mix carob powder in water. Boil, stirring, for 5 minutes, until a smooth paste is formed. Add and Mix well:

1 c peanut butter   **1 c walnuts, chopped**

½ c coconut, shredded,   **1 t vanilla**
        unsweetened

1 c date butter (1 c
        chopped dates
        cooked in ½ c
        water until very soft)

Press into square pan. Refrigerate. Cut into squares to serve. Decorate with walnut half on top. Yield: 2 dozen pieces.

CASHEW CREAM OR MILK

Blend until smooth:

1 c cashews, raw   **½ t vanilla**

1 c hot water   **dash of salt**

8 dates

Cool before serving. For milk, use 3 to 4 cups water.

COMPANY OATMEAL

2 c rolled oats   **⅛ t coriander plus**

1 lg apple, unpeeled,   **¹⁄₁₆ tsp. cardamom**
        cored & sliced
                                  1 tsp. vanilla plus
¼ c coconut, unsweetened   **⅛ t coconut extract**

¼ c nuts, chopped   **1 t salt**

¾ c raisins   **4 c water**

Stir seasonings into water. Combine all ingredients. Bake for 1 hour at 350°.

COOL AND CREAMY OATMEAL

Combine and refrigerate overnight:

2 c oatmeal, raw	**1 c nuts, chopped or**
2 c orange juice	**seeds**
	¼ t salt

Just before serving, add 4 cups of any berries or fresh, frozen or canned fruit.

DANISH APPLE CAKE

Using a 9 x 12 inch baking dish, spread 1½ cups dried bread crumbs in the dish. Top with 2 cups applesauce. Repeat layers as above, ending with ½ cup crumbs. Bake 30 minutes at 350°. Serve with Cashew Cream.

DATE APPLE COOKIES

Blend:

1½ c dates	**¾ c cashews, raw**
1½ c hot water	

Add:

2 c apple, finely chopped	**1 t vanilla**
½ c walnuts, chopped	**1 c raisins**
½ t salt	**3 c rolled oats**

Form cookies on baking sheet. Bake at 350° for 25 minutes.

DATE-COCONUT CRUST

Cover 1 cup dates with enough water to blend into a very thick paste. May need to add a few more dates. Add:

½ c coconut,	**1 t lemon or orange**
unsweetened	**rind grated**

Blend. Spoon and spread into pie pan. Don't make it too thick. Press chopped walnuts (or other nuts) all over and freeze.

FROZEN DESSERT

Blend:

2 c apple or pineapple juice

Add *frozen* fruit until very thick. Fruit can be any unsweetened berries and/or bananas. To freeze bananas just peel ripe ones and put in plastic bags. Freeze at once.

FRUIT CAKE - NUMBER 1

In large bowl, soften 3 tablespoons dry yeast in ½ cup warm apple juice. In saucepan, combine:

¾ c **applesauce**	1 c **apple juice**

Place over low heat to remove chill. Add to yeast mixture. Stir in:

½ c **nut cream***	1½ c **rye flour**
1½ c **whole wheat flour**	1 t **salt**

Mix together:

1 c **prunes, pitted & cut**	½ t **lemon rind**
1 c **dried apricots, cut**	½ c **sesame seeds**
1 c **dates, cut**	½ c **nuts or sunflower**
½ t **ground anise seed**	**seeds**

Mix thoroughly with batter. Place in Pam-sprayed fruit cake or miniature bread pans to ¾ inch of top. Decorate tops with dried fruit flowers made by cutting dried apricots into several petal shaped pieces surrounding a round center. Set in warm place.

When risen to top of pans, bake at 350° for 1 hour. (Turn heat down to 325° for the last 15 minutes if browned sufficiently.) Yield: 4 small ¾ pound loaves.

*Nut cream is made by whizzing 1 cup water and ½ cup raw nuts in blender until smooth.

FRUIT CAKE - NUMBER 2

2 c **white raisins**	½ c **orange juice**
6 c **dried fruit, chopped** **(any combination of peaches, pears, etc.)**	2 c **date butter***
	1 c **soy flour**
	2 c **whole wheat flour**
2 c **walnuts, chopped**	1 c **cashew butter**
2 c **pineapple, crushed & juice**	

Mix well and put in small loaf pans. Bake for 2½ hours at 275°.

*Date butter is made by blending 1½ cups dates and ½ cup hot water together.

FRUIT CANDY

1 c figs, dried, (about
        ¼ lb.)

1 c dates, pitted

1 c raisins

1 c apricots, dried

3 T lemon juice

1 c nuts (walnuts,
        pecans, or almonds)

1 t lemon or orange
        rind, grated

Grind fruits and nuts together through fine blade of food grinder. Then add juice and rind. Line a pan with waxed paper. Pack fruit mixture well and smooth the top. Place a weight on top and let stand for a few hours. Then cut into squares. Decorate tops with shredded coconut or walnut halves.

Optional additions: May add 1 cup peanut butter, ½ cup granola cereal to fruit after grinding. Store in refrigerator or freezer.

FRUIT DELICACY

Grind coarsely:

1 c dates

1 c apricots, dried

1 c raisins

1 c coconut, fresh,
        unsweetened

1 c walnuts

Form into small balls.

FRUITED OATS

Cook for 15 minutes:

4 c water

1 t salt

2 c rolled oats,
        large cooking

Add 2 cups dried fruit; let mixture set until fruit has plumped. You can also use 4 cups fresh or canned fruit.

FRUIT MEDLEY

Combine:

orange sections

grapes, seeded

apples, chopped

strawberries, whole
    or half

banana slices

pineapple chunks
    w/juice

FRUIT WHIP

Soak the dried fruit in fruit juice until puffy 3 cups dried fruit (any single kind or combination). Put 3 lemon slices in soaking water. Blend fruit and liquid until smooth and creamy. Serve over brown rice or cereal or bread.

GRANOLA

Combine and mix well:

10 c oatmeal, raw   **1 c sunflower seeds**
1 c coconut,   **1 t salt**
   unsweetened   **2 c apple or pear sauce**

Spread on cookie sheets and dry completely in a 200 degree oven. It takes several hours.

GRANOLA DESSERTS

Number 1:

Combine equal amounts of any fruit sauce and granola and let stand several hours.

Number 2:

Combine and mix well:

2 c peanut butter   **2 c hot water**
Add:
1 c sesame seeds   **4 c granola**

HAYSTACKS

Blend until smooth:

3 c dates   **½ c orange or**
¼ c hot water   **pineapple juice**
1½ c raisins
Add:
4 c coconut, unsweetened   **⅓ c oatmeal, raw**
¾ c whole wheat flour   **½ t salt**
1⅔ c walnuts, chopped

Put tablespoonfuls on cookie sheets and bake at 300 degrees for 20 to 25 minutes. Watch closely as they burn easily.

JOHNNY APPLESEED RICE PUDDING

½ c brown rice, raw	⅛ t salt
2 c apple juice	½ c raisins

Combine and bring to a boil. Cover and cook on low heat for 40 minutes.

1 c dates, chopped	1½ c apples, diced

Add and cook 10 minutes longer. Top with nuts and serve plain or with nut cream. Yield: 6 servings.

LEMON PUDDING OR PIE

Blend:

1 c pineapple juice, warm	¼ c water
1 c orange juice, warm	1 T cornstarch
4 T lemon juice	¼ t salt
14 dates	¼ c cashews, raw

Cook until thickened. Cool.

LEMON SAUCE

3 t lemon juice	3 T cornstarch
2 c water	½ c apple juice concentrate
1 t lemon rind, grated	

Cook until thick and clear. Serve warm or cold.

NO-SUGAR APPLE PIE

12 oz apple juice concentrate, canned, frozen	1 t cinnamon or cardamom
3 T cornstarch or arrowroot powder	5 lg apples, sweet eating, (i.e., Golden Delicious) peeled and sliced
pinch of salt	

Combine juice, cornstarch, cinnamon, and salt. Heat until thickened. Add sliced apples and simmer until partially cooked. Pour into un-baked pie shell and cover with top crust or crumb topping. Bake at 350° for 45 minutes.

ORANGE SAUCE

2 c orange juice

2 t orange rind, grated

½ t celery salt

2 T cornstarch

Heat until thickened. Serve hot on squash, sweet potatoes, or cold on fruit salad.

PEAR DELIGHT

Blend and serve hot or cold:

1 c almonds

1 c hot water

1 T lemon juice

1 t vanilla

1 c dates

1 t lemon peel

1 c apricots, dried

Serve over pear halves (fresh or canned) and top with chopped almonds.

PINEAPPLE TAPIOCA PUDDING

1½ c pineapple juice

¼ c Minute Tapioca

1 c pineapple, crushed

dash of salt

Mix all ingredients in saucepan; let stand for 5 minutes. Bring to a good boil over medium heat, stirring frequently. Cool 20 minutes and stir. Store in refrigerator. Makes six ½ cup servings.

POLYNESIAN BARS

Mix and cook until consistency of jam:

2 c dates, chopped

1 can pineapple, crushed (20 oz.)

Mix together:

1½ c oatmeal, raw

½ c millet flour

1 c coconut, unsweetened

½ c nuts, chopped

½ t salt

1 c orange juice

Spread ¾ of the oat mixture in a 9 x 12 inch pan. Add date pineapple mixture and top with the remaining oat mixture. Pat down. Bake at 325° for 30 minutes.

PUMPKIN PIE FILLING OR PUDDING

Blend:

½ c cashews, raw	1½ c hot water
2 c dates	2 T cornstarch

Add and mix well:

1 can pumpkin(Lg.)	1 t vanilla
1 t salt	2 t cinnamon

Bake at 350° for 30 minutes.

RAISIN-APPLE PIE FILLING

1 c raisins	2 T arrowroot powder
4 c apples, dried	(or cornstarch)
½ c dates	2 t orange rind, grated
pinch of salt	½–1 c orange juice, fresh

9 inch pie shell, baked

Wash raisins in colander; drain. Cook raisins, apples, dates, salt, orange juice until apples are tender. Moisten arrowroot with 1 tablespoon water; add to hot fruit and stir gently. Cook over low heat until glaze is clear. Add grated orange rind; stir gently. Cool and pour into baked pie shell. Serve warm or cold.

RASPBERRY DESSERT

Thaw and drain 2 quarts frozen raspberries. Heat and blend the juice and 1½ cups dates, or 1 2 ounces frozen apple juice concentrate. Add the berries to the juice and pour over 6 cups fresh whole wheat bread, cubed. This can be served hot or cold.

For a strawberry or blueberry dessert, heat 12 ounces apple juice concentrate (for blueberry use grape juice) and pour over berries and bread cubes.

RAW APPLESAUCE

½ c pineapple juice	2 Golden Delicious apples

Put juice in blender. Wash apples and remove stem and blossomed. Cut in pieces. Add to juice in blender; blend until smooth. Makes delicious sauce served plain, over French toast, or in sherbet glasses with crushed nuts on top. Four pitted dates may be added while blending, if desired.

RICE PUDDING

Mix in a bowl:

½ c peanut butter	2 c apple juice

Add:

2 c raisins or dates, chopped	4 c brown rice, cooked

Put in a baking dish and bake in the oven for 30 minutes at 375°.

SCALLOPED APPLES

Combine:

4 c whole wheat bread crumbs, fresh	6 c apples, chopped raw

Blend and add:

1 c dates, packed	½ c cashews, raw
1 c hot water	

Bake for 45 minutes at 325°. Serve with Fruit Sauce.

FRUIT SAUCE

Combine and blend:

12 oz apple juice concentrate	1½ hot water lemon peel, grated
½ c cashews, raw	2 T cornstarch
2 T lemon juice	

Heat mixture until thick.

SCANDINAVIAN FRUIT SOUP

Combine and heat:

2½ fruits, dried, chopped	1 qt apple juice
½ t anise	2 c orange juice
½ lemon, sliced thin	1 can pineapple chunks with juice
1 c raisins	

Thicken with tapioca or cornstarch.

SESAME BARS - NUMBER 1

Blend:

2 c dates	**1½ c hot water**
1 c cashews, raw	

Add:

1 c coconut, unsweetened	**2 c sesame seeds**
1 c sunflower seeds	

Bake at 300° for 30 minutes.

SESAME BARS - NUMBER 2

Mix:

1½ c date butter	**½ c sunflower seeds**
½ c cashew meal	**1 c sesame seeds**
½ c coconut	

Bake at 300° for 20 to 30 minutes.

SHERBET

Blend:

1 c orange juice concentrate	**1 c water**
	6 bananas, ripe

Add, folding in carefully, 1 can crushed pineapple. Freeze in ice cube trays.

STEAMED PUDDING

Soak overnight in enough apple juice just to cover:

1 c raisins	**1 c apricots, prunes, and apples, chopped dried**

Blend:

1 c hot water	**½ c cashews, raw**
10 dates	

Combine with dried fruit and juice mixture:

½ t salt	**2 c whole wheat flour**
2 c whole wheat bread crumbs, fresh	**2 T lemon rind, grated**
	nut milk

Put all in a Pam-sprayed tube pan and steam 2 hours in a covered steamer, cool, unmold, slice and serve topped with warm or cold apple sauce.

TAPIOCA DESSERTS

Thicken 1 quart of any fruit juice with tapioca or tapioca flour. Cool and add 1 quart of fruit.

TROPICAL FRUIT SALAD

Combine:

**chunks of fresh
pineapple**

papayas, cubed

**bananas, diagonally
sliced**

fresh lime wedges

YUMMY COOKIE BARS

Blend:

2 c dates

**2 c apple juice
concentrate, warm**

Add and mix well:

2 t vanilla

1 c peanut butter

Add and mix:

1 c nuts, chopped

1 c raisins

2 c rolled oats

**1 c coconut,
unsweetened**

3 c whole wheat flour

¾ c soy flour

Spread about one inch deep in baking pans and bake at 300° for 30 to 45 minutes. Cut in bars while still warm.

Write your extra recipes here:

Gravies

BROWN GRAVY

6–8 T whole wheat flour,
          depending on
          thickness desired

2 c cold water

½ t salt

2 t soy sauce

¼ t onion salt

⅛ t garlic salt

⅛ t celery salt

1 t onion, minced,
        dehydrated

Combine flour and water and stir until well blended. Cook over low heat until thick. Add remaining ingredients and cook slowly for 5 to 10 minutes, stirring occasionally.

CASHEW GRAVY

Blend until smooth:

2 c hot water

¾ c cashews, raw

1 T Brewer's yeast

½ t onion powder

½ t garlic powder

Add chicken-style seasoning (See pg. 40) or beef-style seasoning to taste. Heat just to boiling.

ONION GRAVY

Dice 2 large onions. Mix water and soy sauce to make 4 cups, the flavor you want. Simmer 30 minutes. Thicken with cornstarch. Add sliced mushrooms and/or sliced olives, if desired.

QUICK TOMATO GRAVY

¼ t Italian herb
        seasoning

¼ t cumin

3 c tomato juice

½ t onion powder
        or 1 T dried onion

2 T cornstarch

Cook until thick.

Write your extra recipes here:

Jams and Fruit Relishes

APPLE BUTTER

Blend:

12 oz apple juice, warm   **1 t cinnamon or
                                          cardamom**

Add dried apples until thick.

APRICOT JAM

Blend:

2 c pineapple juice, warm   **1 c dates**

Add dried apricots until thick.

APRICOT-PINEAPPLE BUTTER

Blend:

4 lbs apricots, fresh   **2 c dates**

(Should make 7 cups puree.) Add:

1 can pineapple, crushed

Simmer, stirring constantly, until thickened.

BERRY JAM

Blend:

2 c berries, fresh or thawed

Add dried apples while blender is going, until mixture is thick.

COOKED CRANBERRY SAUCE

Cook:

1 pkg cranberries, fresh,   **12 oz apple juice
        raw**   **concentrate**

**6 oz orange juice
        concentrate**

Sieve and thicken with tapioca flour or cornstarch. Cool before serving.

CRANBERRY RELISH

Grind:

1 pkg cranberries, fresh, raw   **2 oranges, unpeeled**
 4 lg apples, cored

Add 12 oz of apple juice from concentrate. Let stand 24 hours before serving.

DATE JAM

 1 c raisins   **1 c water**
 1 c dates

Blend.

PEACH OR PEAR JAM

Blend 12 oz. warm apple juice, add dried peaches or pears until thick.

PRUNE JAM

Blend 12 ounces warm orange juice adding dried prunes until thick.

RAISIN JAM

Blend:
 2 c grape juice, warm   **½ c almonds**
 2 c raisins   **1 t cardamom or**
                                        cinnamon

RASPBERRY JAM

1 c grape, apple, or   **1½ T cornstarch**
     pineapple juice   **1¼–1½ c boysenberries**
 8 chopped dates   **raspberries or**
                                        blueberries

Puree first 3 ingredients and bring to a boil; cook gently for 5 to 8 minutes. Then add berries. If the juice isn't the color of the berries, puree ¼ cup with the juice.

SYRUP

Blend:
 2 c fruit juice   **10 dates**
 1 T cornstarch

Cook to thicken and serve hot or cold on French toast, waffles, or toasted whole grain bread.

Main Dishes

HOW TO COOK DRY BEANS

Method 1:

Sort beans carefully. Wash with cold water in colander. Add beans to boiling water in large kettle. Bring to full boil. Turn off heat. Let stand for an hour or more. Bring to boiling and let boil until tender (about an hour). Add salt and simmer until well done.

Note: There is some evidence that beans cooked by this method cause less flatulence (gas).

Method 2:

Soak beans overnight. Drain. Add drained beans to rapidly boiling water. Heat to boiling point. Boil gently until tender; add salt. Simmer until well done.

Note: Some have found that 1 teaspoon unflavored meat tenderizer, 1 part dry papaya in the tenderizer, contains the enzymes which change the hulls of the beans so they do not cause gas in the intestines. Hot water inactivates the enzymes, so should not be used for soaking beans.

To one cup of beans, add 3 to 4 cups water. For lentils, use 3 cups only. Lentils and split peas may be cooked in one-half hour, and should not be soaked. Black, pinto, great northern, kidney and navy beans cook in about 3 to 5 hours, or 45 minutes in a pressure cooker. Soy beans and garbanzos will take five to eight hours to be palatable and tender, or one hour and twenty minutes in a pressure cooker. To be digested well, beans need to be cooked until hulls have burst and beans are very tender. Overnight cooking in a crock pot works well.

Note: Add salt during very last part of the cooking time. Some feel this helps to reduce the distress factor.

Combinations of legumes and grains make a perfect protein such as peanut butter (a legume) on whole grain bread.

BAKED BEANS

Combine:

4 c navy beans, cooked   **1 c tomato paste**

1 c onion, chopped

Blend and add:

1 c dates, pitted   **¾ c hot water**

Bake 2 hours at 300°.

BAKED NUT RICE

2 c brown rice, cooked   ½ c water

½ c peanut butter, creamy   2 T onion, dried

Bake at 375° until hot, about 20 to 30 minutes. You can add 1 cup dried fruit or 2 cups fresh fruit instead of the onion for a fruit meal.

BEANS AND RICE

Equal amounts of each ingredient:

brown rice, cooked   corn, frozen, fresh
                              or canned
red beans, cooked

                              tomato sauce

Season this dish with cumin and garlic powder for a Mexican flavor.

CARROT RICE

Combine:

2 c carrots, raw, grated   1 c whole wheat crumbs

1 c brown rice, millet or   1 c tomato juice
     barley, cooked   1 c olives, chopped

½ c onion, raw, grated   1 t sage

1 c nuts, chopped   1 t salt

Bake for 1 hour at 325°.

CASHEW VEGETABLE DISH

Combine and saute in ⅓ cup water:

½ c onions, diced   ½ c mushrooms, chopped,
                                   fresh(opt.)
½ c celery, diced

Add:

2 c garbanzos or   1 T chicken-style
     limas, cooked   seasoning
     and lightly mashed   (See pg. 40)

¼ c parsley, chopped   1 c cashews, chopped,
                                   raw
1 t sweet basil

Heat and serve.

CRACKED WHEAT AND ALMOND PILAF

2 c Ala* bulgar wheat or
       cracked wheat
1 c celery, chopped
8 green onions,
    sliced fine
2 c broth or bouillon,
     (vegetable)

2 c water, boiling
1 c almonds, raw, sliced
1½ t salt
¼ t marjoram
½ t oregano

Brown celery and onions lightly in Pam-sprayed pan; add Ala and brown. Place in a 2 quart casserole and pour bouillon and boiling water over top. Blend in almonds, salt, marjoram and oregano. Cover and bake in a 325° oven for 1½ hours.

Note: If you have a blender or a flour mill, you can combine three of four whole grains (such as wheat, rye, brown rice, and barley) and crack them yourself for this recipe. Combining several whole grains together enhances the protein quality and provides more abundant supplies of all nutrients.

*Ala can be found in your local supermarket under the trade name of Fisher's Ala. It should be located with the brown rice and other grain items.

GARDEN RICE

Combine and cook only until the spinach wilts:

1 lb spinach, fresh,
      sliced
1 c water chestnuts,
     sliced
¼ c water

½ c green onions,
     finely diced
½ c celery, finely diced

Stir in:

2 c brown rice, cooked
¼ t rosemary

1 t chicken-style
     seasoning
     (See pg. 40)

Heat and serve.

GLUTEN

Mix and let stand (covered) for 1 hour:

2 c Do-Pep   **3 c warm water**

1 c whole wheat flour

Broth: Mix in a large baking pan with a cover:

1½ c old-fashioned   **6 c warm water**
      peanut butter   **⅓ c soy sauce**

Divide the gluten into small pieces and put Into the broth. Bake at 300° for one hour.

HERB RICE

1 c brown rice   **½ c onion, chopped**

2 c tomato juice   **¼ c parsley, chopped**

½ t celery salt   **½ t lemon peel, grated**

¼ t oregano, rosemary
      and thyme

Combine and cook according to rice directions.

LENTILS AND RICE

Combine equal amounts:

brown rice, cooked   **lentils, cooked**

Add onions, chopped and cooked (about ½ of the measured amount of brown rice or lentils). This will need little or no salt.

LENTIL ROAST

Soak 4 cups cubed bread In 1 cup nut milk. Add:

2 c lentils, cooked   **¾ t sage**

¾ c nuts, chopped   **½ chopped onion**

1 t salt

Bake 1 hour at 325°.

MACARONI AND CASHEW NUT "CHEESE" SAUCE

Cook:

1 c macaroni, enriched,   **1 qt water, boiling**
      or whole wheat   **½ t salt**

Crumbs:

¼ c whole wheat crumbs   **1 T Brewer's flake yeast**

Sauce:

½ c cashew nuts, raw	1 t salt
2 oz pimentos,(jar)	¼ t onion powder
¼ c lemon juice	dash garlic powder
3 T Brewer's flake yeast	1½ c water

Add macaroni to boiling, salted water. Cook, uncovered, 15 minutes. Mix lightly. Do not drain cooking water. While macaroni is cooking, combine "cheese" sauce ingredients In blender until smooth. Add to macaroni. Salt to taste. Put in casserole; cover. Bake at 350° for 30 minutes. Sprinkle with crumbs and bake, uncovered, for 15 minutes. You can substitute almonds or peanuts for cashew nuts, if desired.

MILLET ENTREE

1 c millet, uncooked	½ c olives, ripe, sliced
5 c tomato juice	½ c cashew pieces
1 med onion, chopped	½ t sage
½ t salt	½ T garlic powder or savory

Mix in the same entree dish used for baking. Cover well with foil or well fitting lid so the moisture from the entree won't escape. Bake at 325° for 2 hours, then bake at 250° for 1 more hour.

Note: This entree' is delicious without gravy.

POTTAGE

Mix:

1 c lentils, dry	2 c water
½ c brown rice, uncooked	1 c mushrooms (opt)

Blend and add:

1 c olives	1 med onion, raw
¾ c water	

Cook on low heat until done, about 45 minutes.

RICE STUFFING

3 c brown rice,
    millet or barley,
    cooked

1 c celery, diced

1 c onion, diced

1 c mushrooms, sliced
    (opt.)

½ c nut butter

1 T soy sauce

2 t sage

Add whole grain bread crumbs for desired consistency. Bake as a loaf or stuff peppers, eggplant, or acorn squash. Bake at 350° F for 45 minutes.

SESAME SEED PILAF

Cook until rice is done:

1 lg onion, chopped

1 garlic clove, minced

1 c brown rice

2 c water

1 T chicken-style
    seasoning
    (See pg. 40)

Add 1 package (10 ounces) thawed frozen peas and ½ cup toasted sesame seeds. Mix and top with ¼ cup sesame seeds.

SOYBEAN SOUFFLE

Soak overnight:

1½ c soybeans

Drain, then blend thoroughly, soybeans,

1 onion

2½ c warm water

Add:

2 t salt

1 t garlic powder

1½ c rolled wheat, oats
    or barley

Bake 2 hours at 300°. Serve with onion or tomato gravy.

SOYTEENA

1 c soy beans, dry
    (2½ to 3 c. soaked
    and drained)

2 c water

1 c tomato juice

½ c peanut butter

2 t salt

1 celery stalk

¼ c yeast flakes

½ med onion

4 T soy sauce
    garlic salt to taste

1 c cornmeal

Combine all the ingredients, except the cornmeal, and put in blender until smooth, Remove from blender; add cornmeal. Pour into Pam-sprayed Number 2 cans and steam for 2 hours, or longer. (For slightly firmer texture, cover cans with foil and rubber bands.) Steam in large kettle about half full of water when cans are set in it. *Keep water simmering with lid* on. When cooled, remove from cans. Slice and serve on sandwiches.

TOMATO-LENTIL ON BREAD

Cook 30 minutes

2 c lentils, uncooked	**½ t cumin**
1 c onions, chopped	**¼ oregano**
1 c carrot, diced	**1 t salt**
4 c tomato juice	

Pour over 3 cups fresh whole wheat bread crumbs. Bake for 30 minutes at 300°.

TOMATOES AND RICE

Mix in a bowl:

2 c brown rice, cooked	**1 can green beans, cut**
1 c tomatoes, chopped	**1 t onion salt**
1 c black olives, chopped	

Put in a baking dish and bake 30 minutes at 350°.

VEGETABLE CASSEROLE

Combine:

1 eggplant, cubed	**2 c garbanzos, cooked**
½ garlic salt	**16 oz tomato paste**
3 sm zucchini, sliced	**¼ c parsley, chopped**
3 med onions, thinly sliced	**1 t Italian herb seasoning**
2 c kidney beans, cooked	

Bake at 375° for about 45 minutes, until vegetables are fork tender.

WALNUT-RICE STUFFING

1 lg onion, chopped

1 c brown rice

¼ c parsley, minced

1¾ c water

2 T lemon juice

salt as needed

1 t oregano

½ t thyme

scooped out portion
of tomatoes,
zucchini, or
eggplant

Cook above ingredients. When rice is done, add 1 cup of chopped walnuts. Use to stuff or fill tomatoes, zucchini, eggplant, or green peppers. (About 12 med. tomatoes, 2 lg. eggplants, 6 med. zucchini, or 8–10 med. green peppers.) Bake, uncovered, at 350° 30 minutes.

WALNUT STUFFING BALLS

Combine:

4 c bread crumbs

½ c onion, finely
chopped or grated

1 t celery seed

½ c parsley, chopped

1 c walnuts, course
chopped

½ c nut butter

½ t salt

1 t sage

Add just enough seasoned water [1½ teaspoons chicken-style seasoning (See pg. 40) to 1 cup hot water] to form 2 inch balls. Bake on cookie sheets at 375° for about 15 minutes, until crisp and brown.

ZUCCHINI - PEANUTS - BARLEY

Cook 1 cup barley in 3 cups vegetable broth or tomato juice. Cook separately until crisp and tender:

4 med zucchini, cut in
julienne strips

1 c water

1½ t chicken-style
seasoning
(See pg. 40)

Add 1½ cups coarsely ground peanuts. Thicken slightly with cornstarch and serve over the barley.

ZUCCHINI-RICE CASSEROLE

5 c zucchini, thinly
sliced

1 c onion, finely chopped

2 tomatoes, chopped

½t garlic salt

½ t sweet basil

½ t oregano

1 c brown rice

1 c water

Combine above ingredients. Bake for 40 minutes at 350 degrees.

Patties

BEAN-OAT PATTIES

Mash 1 cup cooked beans (any kind) in liquid in which they were cooked. Add and mix well:

1 c rolled oats	**½ c onion, chopped**
½ c nuts, chopped	**½ t sage**
2 T food yeast	**salt to taste**

Shape into patties and bake for 30 minutes at 350°. Turn after 15 minutes. Serve with tomato sauce or onion gravy.

BILLY BURGERS

2 c barley, cooked	**¼ c walnuts, ground**
½ c potato, raw, grated	**½ t thyme**
1 onion, chopped	**salt**

Add enough bread crumbs so patties hold together. Bake at 325° for 30 minutes.

GARBANZO-RICE PATTIES

Blend:

1½ c garbanzos, soaked and drained	**1 sm onion**
	1 T soy sauce
½ c cashews, raw	**1¼ c hot water**

Add:

1½ c brown rice, cooked	**1 T Brewer's yeast**
¼ t garlic powder	

Form patties on cookie sheets and bake 30 minutes at 325°.

LENTIL PATTIES

Combine and mix well:

2 c lentils, well cooked	**2½ c whole wheat bread crumbs or cooked brown rice**
1 c onion, chopped	
½ c walnuts, ground	
1 t salt	**½ t sage**
	2 T soy sauce

Add enough nut milk to form patties. Place on a cookie sheet and bake 30 minutes at 325°.

LENTIL RICE PATTIES

2 c lentils, cooked

2 c brown rice, cooked

½ onion, chopped

1 t sage

salt as needed

1 c crumbs nut milk
to moisten if needed

Mix together. Place on cookie sheet. Bake 20 minutes at 350°.

MEATLESS HAMBURGERS

1 c walnuts, chopped

1 c olives, blended

2 c rolled oats

1 onion, chopped

1 t salt

1 T soy sauce

½ t sage

½ t thyme

¼ t marjoram

2 c nut milk

½ t garlic powder

½ t onion salt

Mix together all ingredients. Let stand 15 to 20 minutes. Form Into patties and brown about 15 minutes on each side in skillet over medium heat, or In oven for 30 minutes at 325°.

MILLET PATTIES—1

Blend:

½ c cashews, raw

1 c hot water

Add and mix well:

1½ c millet, cooked

½ c whole wheat flour

1 T soy sauce

½ c onion, chopped

½ t garlic powder

¼ c soy flour

salt to taste

Form patties and bake 30 minutes at 325°.

MILLET PATTIES—2

Blend:

2 c hot water

1 onion

1 c cashews, raw

Add:

3 c millet, cooked

½ c soy flour

½ t garlic powder

1 c cornmeal

1 t sage

1 t salt

Form patties and bake on cookie sheets 30 minutes at 325°. Turn once.

OATMEAL-WHEAT GERM PATTIES

1½ c oatmeal, uncooked

1 c wheat germ

1 pkg yeast, dry in ¼ c water or 1 T dry yeast

4 t soy sauce

1 t salt

1½ c nut milk

pinch of sage

dash of garlic powder

1 onion, chopped

8 t soy flour, with 8 t water

¼ c nuts, chopped

Dissolve yeast in water and mix all ingredients together. Form into patties and bake on Pam sprayed cookie sheet in a 350° oven until brown, 20 to 30 minutes. Place patties in casserole dish and cover with favorite brown gravy or onion gravy and bake for 45 minutes at 350°.

SAVORY SOYBEAN PATTIES

3 c water

⅔ c soybeans, dry

1¼ c water

1⅓ c rolled oats

1 sm onion, chopped or 1 t onion powder

1 t Italian herb seasoning

2 T soy sauce

½ t salt

1 T Brewer's type yeast (opt.)

Soak soybeans overnight In 3 cups water. Drain. Blend soybeans in 1¼ cups water until quite fine. Remove to bowl and add seasonings and rolled oats. Allow to stand 10 minutes for rolled oats to absorb moisture. Stir again and drop by rounded tablespoons on cookie sheet. Cook until lightly browned. Turn and cook until lightly browned. Reduce heat to 275° and allow to cook 10 minutes longer. Serve with tomato gravy. Bake at 325°.

SPROUTED WHEAT BURGERS

2 c sprouted wheat

½ c sunflower seeds,
　　　ground or chopped

½ c pumpkin seeds,
　　　ground or chopped

2 c barley or millet,
　　　cooked

½ c bread crumbs, soft

2 T peanut butter

2 T soy sauce

1 T onion powder or

¼ c onion, raw, chopped

½ t thyme

½ t salt

½ t sage

Mold with hands to form patties. Brown on both sides. Place between burger buns and serve with homemade catsup. Or serve with gravy as a meatless main dish. Bake in oven at 325° for 30 minutes.

VEGEBURGERS

Cook and grind:

4 c soybeans

2 c garbanzos

Add:

3 c brown rice, cooked

2 onions, chopped

1 T sage

1 t celery salt

2 T chicken-style
　　　seasoning
　　　(See pg. 40)

1 t garlic powder

If dry, add bean stock. If wet, add crumbs or oatmeal. Form patties and bake, covered with foil, for 25 minutes at 350°, then turn and bake 10 minutes or more.

Pickles

BEAN RELISH

Combine:

6 c red beans, cooked	**2 cans corn with liquid**

Set aside. In a saucepan, combine:

½ c dates	**3 onions, chopped**
1 c water	**1 t salt**
2 c lemon juice	**2 t celery seed**

Cook until onions are tender. Thicken with cornstarch and pour over beans and corn. Chill 4 hours or overnight.

BREAD AND BUTTER PICKLES

Let stand 4 hours:

4 qt cucumbers, thinly sliced, unpeeled	**1 qt onions, sliced**
	½ salt

Drain well. In large kettle, combine:

2 cans pineapple juice (lg.)	**2 T celery salt**
2 c lemon juice	**1 T dill seed**
1 t turmeric	**4 garlic cloves**

Bring juices to a boil and add cucumbers, onions, and heat. Put in hot, clean jars and water bath in canner for 5 minutes.

DILLS

Boil and cool 16 cups of water and 1 cup salt. Set aside to cool. Soak cucumbers in plain cold water overnight. Scrub with a brush and soak 1 hour more in clean water.

Pack cucumbers in quart jars with 3 garlic cloves, sliced, 1 head fresh dill, and 3 carrot sticks.

Add salt water and seal. Leave in a warm room for at least 3 weeks before using.

PICKLED VEGETABLES

Cook until just tender, vegetables such as beets, carrots, turnips, cauliflower, or broccoli.

Put beets alone, but other vegetables can be combined. Also you can add raw cucumbers, zucchini, and onion rings one hour before serving.

Cover vegetables with the following:

12 oz apple juice concentrate	**1 garlic clove**
¾ c lemon juice	**1 t dill seed**
1 c hot water	**1 t celery seed**

Chill several hours.

Write your extra recipes here:

Salads

ABC SALAD

4 lg apples, diced
2 bananas, diced

1 c celery, finely
chopped or sliced

Add Coleslaw Dressing.

AVOCADO SALAD

¼ c lemon juice
2 lg avocados, cubed
4 green onions, sliced

1 sm cauliflower head,
coarsely grated

BEAN KRAUT SALAD

kidney beans

garbanzo beans

onion rings

black olives

green peppers

sauerkraut

Combine; eat as is or put on greens if you wish. The amount of each ingredient is determined by individual taste and quantity desired.

BEAN SLAW

½ med cabbage head,
shredded

1½ c red beans

use coleslaw Dressing.

BROCCOLI SALAD

This broccoli dish can be either vegetable or salad on your menu.

1½ lbs broccoli
boiling, salted water
3 T lemon juice
2 T green onion, minced

¼ t garlic salt
sliced radishes for
garnish

Trim off broccoli stem ends and peel outer layer of stalks; cut large spears in half lengthwise. Wash spears well. Immerse in boiling, salted water and cook, uncovered, until just tender when pierced. Drain well; chill up to 24 hours.

For the dressing, combine the lemon juice, green onion, garlic salt, in a small jar; shake well.

About an hour before serving, arrange chilled broccoli spears on 6 lettuce-lined salad plates. Spoon dressing evenly over each; garnish with the radishes.

BRUSSELS SPROUTS SALAD

Put Coleslaw Dressing on hot cooked Brussels sprouts. Chill several hours. Add cherry tomatoes and sliced green onions just before serving,

CABBAGE

4 c cabbage, shredded	**½ c onion, finely chopped**
1½ c corn, whole kernel	**1 c olives, chopped**

Add Coleslaw Dressing.

CRISPY SPROUTS SALAD

2 c bean sprouts	**1 c mushrooms, raw,**
2 c alfalfa sprouts	**sliced (opt.)**
½ c green peas, fresh	
or frozen	

Mix; serve with Avocado Dressing.

CUCUMBER SALAD

Overgrown, seedy cucumbers may be cut in half lengthwise and seeds scooped out. Fill centers with finely shredded cabbage or carrots or beets or a combination of vegetables mixed with Lemon Dressing.

FRUIT SALAD

Mix in a pretty bowl:

2 oranges, cut up	**3 bananas, sliced**
2 apples, chopped	**1 can pineapple chunks**
1 c grapes	**with the juice,**
2 c strawberries, cut	**unsweetened**
in half	

No dressing needed.

GARBANZO-PINEAPPLE SALAD

3 c garbanzo beans,	**1 can pineapple chunks**
cooked	**with juice**
10 cherry tomatoes	

Use French Dressing.

GREEN BEAN SALAD

Combine:

green beans   **cherry tomatoes**
onion rings

Add Italian Dressing and mix.

GREEN AND GOLD SALAD

3 c zucchini, shredded   **½ c green onions, sliced**
3 c carrots, shredded

Blend and add:

¼ c lemon juice   **½ c dates**
¼ c hot water   **salt as needed**

GREEN PEA SALAD

1 c celery, sliced   **3 c green peas, cooked**
10 cherry tomatoes, cut in half

Use Tomato Dressing.

HOLIDAY SALAD BOWL

This salad could double as the vegetable for a holiday buffet.

1 lb green beans   **16–18 cherry tomatoes,**
water   **halved**
6–8 oz water chestnuts,   **· ½ tsp. dry basil**
drained   **¼ t oregano leaves**
½ lb mushroom (opt.)   **¼ t lemon peel, grated**
8 oz olives, ripe,   **2 t lemon juice**
drained   **garlic salt**

Break off tips from beans; snap into about 2 inch lengths. Bring ½ inch water to a boil in a frying pan with a lid. Add beans, cover, and boil until just tender to bite, 5 to 7 minutes. Drain, plunge into cold water, drain again. Turn into a salad bowl.

Slice water chestnuts and mushrooms; add to beans along with olives and tomatoes. Add basil, oregano, and lemon peel and juice; pour over vegetables and mix well. Season with garlic salt to taste. Cover and chill as long as overnight.

LETTUCE TOMATO SALAD

Blend:

2 c cashews, raw

1 c water

2 T parsley

½ c green onions, sliced

⅓ c celery or 1 T celery seed

½ c radishes, chopped

½ c carrot, shredded

½ t garlic salt

½ t dill seed

1 t turmeric

Chill several hours and serve on green lettuce leaves and tomato slices.

LIMA BEAN SALAD

2 c green limas, cooked

1 c celery, chopped

2 c green peas, cooked

Dressing:

1½ c pineapple juice

2 T lemon juice

1 t onion powder

1 t celery salt

MACARONI SALAD

3 c macaroni, cooked

1 c olives, ripe, chopped

2 lg tomatoes, chopped

2 c garbanzo beans

1 c green onions, sliced

2 c whole kernel corn

1 c green peas

Use Coleslaw Dressing.

MAIN COURSE SALAD

3 c salad greens, torn

1 carrot, thinly sliced or coarsely grated

½ c peanuts, chopped

3 T parsley, chopped

2 T wheat germ

2 T sunflower seeds

1 avocado, cubed

1 c radishes, chopped
      onion rings

Use Cucumber Dressing.

MANY BEAN SALAD

Use several beans (such as northern, garbanzo, red, plus whole string green and wax beans). Green pepper rings and onion rings, (white and red) are optional. A sprinkle of fresh lemon juice and salt is enough dressing.

MINT-AVOCADO SALAD

Mix:

½ c cashew cream

3 T mint, fresh, finely
     chopped

2 T lemon juice

1 t salt

Add to:

3 lg avocados (cut in
      chunks)

2 bananas, sliced

1 can pineapple chunks
       with juice

MOCK CRAB SALAD

Grind:

2 c parsnips, raw

1 c carrots, raw

½ c onions, raw

10 olives, ripe

Moisten with Golden Sauce and serve on salad greens.

PEANUT, CARROT, RICE SALAD

Blend:

½ c peanut butter

½ c hot water

½ c dates

Add:

4 c brown rice, cooked

2 c carrots, shredded

Serve on lettuce.

POTATO SALAD

6 potatoes, cooked,
   cubed

1 med cucumber, thinly
       sliced

1 sm onion, thinly sliced

Dressing:

1 c water

1 T chicken-style
     seasoning (See pg. 40)

1 t dill seed

½ c cashews

1 T lemon juice

     salt as needed

Blend dressing ingredients; mix lightly and chill several hours.

RICE SALAD

Combine:

2 c brown rice, cooked	**½ c green onions, chopped**
½ c carrot, shredded	**½ c cucumber, diced**

Dressing:

Blend:

¼ c lemon juice	**½ t salt**
½ c water	**4 dates**

Serve on lettuce leaves and top with sesame seeds.

ROSY CRUNCH SALAD

1 c carrots, raw, shredded	**¼ c sunflower seeds**
1 c beets, raw, shredded	**green pepper strips**
1 c turnips, raw, shredded	**endive or leaf lettuce**

Toss all shredded vegetables together with Italian Dressing and sunflower seeds. Serve on bed of endive or lettuce. Garnish with green pepper strips.

SPINACH SALAD

Combine:

spinach, fresh, shredded	**carrots, thinly, sliced**
lettuce, broken	**zucchini, thinly sliced**
	celery, thinly sliced

Use Sweet Basil Dressing.

"6" THINGS SALAD

Mix in a bowl:

3 c lettuce, torn	**½ c green onion, sliced**
1 c black olives, sliced	**10 cherry tomatoes, cut in half**
1 c brown rice, cooked	
1 c peas, cooked or fresh	

Use Italian Dressing.

SPRING VEGETABLE SALAD

Cook separately until just tender:

potatoes, tiny, whole   **green beans, whole**

Line a salad bowl with lettuce leaves and arrange the above vegetables over them. Add:

garbanzo beans   **tomato wedges**

onion rings   **olives**

Cover and cool several hours. Serve with Avocado Dressing.

TOMATO ASPIC

Combine:

4 T cornstarch   **2 T lemon juice**

¾ t onion salt

Gradually add 2 cups tomato juice. Boil 2 minutes, stirring constantly. Pour in mold and refrigerate. May add celery or olives (sliced thinly).

VEGETABLE SALAD

1 qt lettuce, chopped   **10 radishes, thinly sliced**

3 tomatoes, diced

1 cucumber, thinly sliced   **¼ c parsley, fresh, chopped**

green onions, thinly sliced   **¼ c mint, fresh, chopped**

Dressing:

Blend:

½ c lemon juice   **¼ t garlic salt or 1 garlic clove fresh, finely grated**

¼ c hot water

6 dates

WHITE BEAN SALAD

Blend:

½ c lemon juice   **1 t salt**

½ c hot water   **1 med onion**

6 dates   **½ c cashews, raw**

Pour over 4 cups cooked hot white beans. Cool several hours. Add:

½ c parsley, fresh, chopped   **1 c radishes, sliced**

Serve.

ZIPPY SPINACH TOSS

1 **spinach, bunch,**   ¼ lb **mushrooms, fresh,**
   washed thoroughly   **washed and sliced**
6 **cauliflower flowerettes,**
   thinly sliced

Tear spinach into bite-sized pieces, discarding stems. Toss all ingredients.

For variation, add 1 small sweet red onion, thinly sliced, sliced radishes, carrots or olives.

Write extra recipes here:

Salad Dressing

AVOCADO-CASHEW DRESSING

Blend until smooth:

½ c **cashews, raw**

Add and continue to blend:

1½ c **hot water**   2 t **lemon juice**

2 **avocados**

For dip, add ½ medium size onion to first ingredients.

AVOCADO DRESSING

½ c **orange juice**   ¼ t **salt**

1 T **lemon juice**   1 **avocado, mashed**

COLESLAW DRESSING

2 c **cashews, raw**   1 t **salt**

3 c **pineapple juice**   1 t **onion powder**

⅓ c **lemon juice**

Blend.

CUCUMBER DRESSING

Blend until smooth:

¾ c **cashews, raw**   4 **cucumber, thick slices**

¾ c **hot water**   4 **green onions**

Cool. Add before using:

¼ c **parsley, minced**   1 t **salt and herbs your family likes**

¼ c **radishes, diced**

DRESSING FOR SALADS/COOKED VEGETABLES

Blend:

**2 fresh tomatoes or
2 raw carrots or 10
radishes or 1
cucumber or 1
seeded green pepper**

¼ c water

Add:

onion powder

celery salt

garlic powder

lemon juice

To taste.

FRENCH DRESSING

½ c lemon juice

½ t salt

¼ c cashews, raw

½ t paprika

⅓ c water

**garlic, onion and
dill as desired**

Blend.

ITALIAN DRESSING

⅓ c lemon juice

3 c pineapple juice

1 t celery seed

1 t basil, crushed

1 t onion powder

Mix well and shake before using.

LEMON DRESSING

Blend.

2 T lemon peel, grated

½ c lemon juice

**2 garlic cloves, fine
grated**

1 c tomato juice

½ t coriander

½ t cumin

½ t paprika

½ t turmeric

6 dates

MAYONNAISE (Or Use As Sour Cream)

Thicken 2 cups water with 3 tablespoons cornstarch. Cool slightly.
Blend well:

2 c hot water	**2 c cashews, raw**

Add and blend well:

¾ c lemon juice	**1 T salt**
2 t garlic powder	**2 t onion powder**

Add to the starch mixture and mix thoroughly. Cool before using.

MOCK MAYONNAISE

Blend:

1½ c water	**½ c white flour, unbleached**

Cook over medium heat until thick and bubbly. Cool. Return to
blender and add:

2 T lemon juice	**1 t salt**
6 dates	**⅛ t garlic powder**
⅛ t onion powder	

Blend until creamy. Store in covered container in refrigerator.

Variation: For more zip, add few shakes dill weed, paprika, turmeric
or other herbs.

SWEET BASIL DRESSING

2 T onion, dry	**1 t sweet basil**
1 c hot water	**2 T lemon juice**
½ c cashews, raw	**10 olives**
½ t salt	

Blend.

TOMATO-CASHEW DRESSING

½ c cashews, raw	**1 t marjoram**
½ onion, raw	**2 c tomato juice**
1 t garlic powder	**6 oz apple juice concentrate**
1 t celery salt	**salt If needed**
1 t paprika	

Blend well.

TOMATO DRESSING

½ c tomato juice
2 T lemon juice
1 t onion powder

1 t parsley, dried
1 t food yeast

Put in a jar and shake before using.

Write an extra recipe here:

Sauces

CASHEW CHEESE

1 c water	**1 T agar flakes**

Cook together until clear, 2 or 3 minutes. Pour hot into blender. Add:

1½ cashews, raw	**½ t onion powder**
1 t salt	**sm carrot (for color)**

Blend well; add ¼ cup lemon juice. Store in refrigerator.

CASHEW CHEESE SPREAD

1 c cashews, raw	**¼ c lemon juice**
½ c hot water	**2 oz pimentos(1 can)**
½ t salt	**or 1 carrot, sliced**
½ t garlic powder	**(for color)**
½ t onion powder	

Blend.

LOW FAT CHEESE SPREAD

2 c water	**½ t paprika (opt)**
¼ c Emes Kosher-Jel unflavored	**2 t onion powder**
	½ t garlic powder
2 c corn meal, cooked	**½ c lemon juice (fresh if possible)**
½ c yeast flakes	
1 T salt or 2 T Bragg's Liquid Aminos	

Cook ½ c corn meal in 2 c of water until thick. Soak gelatin in 1 c cold water while corn is cooking. Pour boiling corn meal over gelatin. Add remaining ingredients. Blend mixture. Add one cup cold water and pour into mold. Refrigerate before serving. May be frozen until needed. Do not substitute agar for the Emes Kosher-Jel, as it doesn't give good results. May be used on toast or as spread for bread. It will melt when heated.

CATSUP

Blend:

1 sm onion
1 t garlic powder
¼ c lemon juice

1 c tomato sauce
8 dates

Add:

1 c tomato sauce
1 c 1 tomato paste
1 t salt

1 t paprika
½ t cumin
½ t basil

Simmer for 1 hour, stirring occasionally.

GOLDEN SAUCE

Blend:

1 c potato, cooked, diced
1 lg carrot, cooked
½ c cashews, raw
1 t onion or celery salt

1 c water (from cooked vegetables)
¼ c lemon juice

This is good on cauliflower, broccoli, etc.

NUTEENA-LIKE SANDWICH SPREAD

1¼ c garbanzo beans, cooked, reserve liquid
⅔ c olives, chopped
⅓ c garbanzo liquid
⅓ c peanut butter

1½ T tomato paste
¼ t Brewer's yeast
1⁄16 t onion powder
1⁄16 t lemon juice

Mash garbanzo beans thoroughly. *Mash* in remaining ingredients.

PARMESAN CHEESE

Blend:

1 c sesame seeds

¼ c lemon juice

Add and mix:

1 c Brewer's yeast flakes
1 T onion powder
¼ c Bakon yeast
2 t garlic powder

3 T chicken-style seasoning (See pg. 40)

Store in a covered container in a cool place.

SAUCE FOR GREENS (MUSTARD)

Combine and heat:

½ t thyme	⅓ c lemon juice
2 t vegesalt	1 c water
1 t turmeric	2 T cornstarch

Serve on any greens. For mustard let the above cool a little and blend with 1 cup raw cashews. Use as dressing or dip.

SOYBEAN SPREAD

2 c soybeans, cooked	1 garlic clove
3 T parsley	salt as needed
2 T onion, dried	

Blend.

SPANISH SAUCE

Cook:

4 c onions, coarse chopped	3 c celery, sliced
1 c water	

Add and heat:

1 c mushrooms, sliced	½ T chicken-style
1 c ripe olives, sliced	seasoning
1 c tomatoes, cooked,	(See pg. 40)
mashed	½ t garlic powder
½ t oregano	1 t cumin
2 c tomato paste	

Use on rice, beans, barley, or pasta.

Write your extra recipes here:

Soups and Stews

AUTUMN VEGETABLE CHOWDER

1 c water	chopped parsley
1 med onion, chopped	1 lb tomatoes
1 c carrot, thinly sliced	1 T beef style seasoning
½ c celery, thinly sliced	(McKay's)
2 c potatoes, peeled,	2 c nut milk
diced	salt

In a 3 quart pan, put water and the onion; cook until limp. Stir in the carrot, celery, potatoes, tomatoes and seasoning. Cover and simmer for 35 minutes, stiffing occasionally, or until vegetables are tender when pierced. Gradually stir in milk and heat until piping hot; season to taste with salt. Ladle into mugs or small bowls; sprinkle with parsley.

BEAN SOUP OR STEW

Soak and cook 1 cup dry lima beans, lentils, navy beans, or garbanzo beans until done.

For soup, cut the vegetables small - for stew, use whole vegetables, or cut in chunks. Cook until tender:

2 c carrots	2 med potatoes
2 med onions	1½ qts tomato juice

Combine vegetables and beans and 2 cups peas. Heat and serve.

BLACK BEANS OVER RICE

1 lb black beans	1 bay leaf
1 lg onion, chopped	2 t salt
2 green peppers,	1 lb brown rice, cooked
chopped	green onions,
1 garlic clove, minced	chopped

Cover beans with 6 cups boiling water and let set 1 hour. Drain and add 6 cups fresh cold water. Cook over low heat (gently bubbling) 1 hour. Saute onions, green peppers and garlic in ¼ cup water. Combine with beans; add other seasonings and cook until beans are tender and liquid is thick. Serve over brown rice and top with green onions.

BORSCH

Cook until tender:

5 celery stalks, sliced	**½ t thyme**
2 cabbage heads, sliced	**½ t sage**
	½ t marjoram
2 c onions, diced	**2 T chicken-style seasoning (See pg. 40)**
1 c carrots, sliced	
1 t garlic powder	
1 qt water	**2 T lemon juice**

Blend:

2 c beets, cooked	**1 qt water**

Add to cooked vegetables; heat and serve.

CHILI

6 c chili or pinto beans, cooked	**3 c tomato juice**
	1 t garlic powder
1 c tomato paste	**2 t cumin**

Salt, if needed. Simmer 1 hour.

CHILLED GREEN BEAN BISQUE

⅓ c almonds, slivered	**4 c green beans, in 1 inch pieces (about 1 lb.)**
1 garlic clove, minced or pressed	
1 med onion, chopped	**¼ t savory leaves**
2 c water	**vegesalt to taste**

Toast almonds in a 350° oven for 5 to 7 minutes, or until golden; set aside. Put ¼ cup water in a 3 quart pan, over medium heat; add garlic and onion and saute until limp. Stir in beans and water; cover and simmer 10 minutes, or until beans are tender to bite. Turn mixture into a blender and whirl until smooth; season with savory and salt. Cover and chili well. To serve, pour into chilled mugs, then top each with nuts.

CORN CHOWDER

Cook:

2 c corn, thawed, frozen or canned	**1 c potato, grated, cooked**
1 T chicken-style seasoning (See pg. 40)	**2 c water**
	1 t sweet basil

Add blended:

2 c hot water	**salt if needed**
1 c cashews, raw	

Heat and serve.

CREAMY HERBED WALNUT SOUP

1½ c walnuts, chopped	**1 med onion, sliced**
2 c cashew milk	**2 T flour, all-purpose**
½ bay leaf	**3 c chicken flavored broth**
¼ t thyme leaves	
¼ t dry basil	**¼ c water**
2 T parsley, chopped	**chives or green onions, finely chopped**
½ c celery, thinly sliced	
water	

Cover walnuts with water and bring to a boil; boil for 3 minutes then drain. Pour milk over drained nuts and add bay leaf, thyme, basil, and parsley; heat, but do not boil; cover and set aside for 20 minutes.

Meanwhile, in a 3 quart pan, combine water, onion and celery, and cook about 5 minutes. Blend in the flour and broth; cook, stirring, until soup boils. Reduce heat and simmer gently for 10 minutes, then remove bay leaf and add milk mixture to soup. Whirl soup a small amount at a time in a blender until pureed.

Cover and refrigerate if made ahead. just before serving, reheat to simmering. Sprinkle each serving with chives.

Note: When making chicken flavored broth use Chicken-style seasoning (See pg. 40)

GARBANZOS-ALMONDS

Marinate 2 cups cooked garbanzos in ⅓ cup soy sauce and ⅔ cup water overnight. Combine and cook briefly:

1½ c celery, finely sliced	**1 pkg pea pods, Chinese**
1 c onions, chopped	**2 tomatoes, chopped**
1 can bamboo shoots	**1 T chicken-style**
1 can water chestnuts, sliced	**seasoning (See pg. 40)**
1 c water	

Add drained garbanzos, thicken slightly with cornstarch. Serve over rice and sprinkle with chopped almonds.

GARBANZO SOUP

Blend:

2 c garbanzos, cooked	**½ c lemon juice**
1 t salt	**1 c sesame seeds**
½ t garlic salt or fresh garlic	**2 c water**

Serve chilled.

ICY LEMON SOUP

Blend to make cashew cream:

1 c cashews, raw	**2 c water**

Add:

1 c water	**¾ c lemon juice**
1 T curry*	

Cool several hours and serve with thin lemon slices.

*Curry:

2 T turmeric	**3 bay leaves**
2 T cumin	**¼ t garlic powder**
1 T coriander	**½ t onion powder**

Grind in Moulinex.

LENTIL-RICE SOUP

½ c brown rice	**1 can tomatoes (large)**
1 c lentils, dry	**1–1½ t salt to taste**
2 qts water	**2 T soy sauce**
1 lg onion, chopped	

Mix and cook slowly until all Ingredients are tender. Sometimes more liquid is needed. Add tomato juice for more liquid. Thyme or oregano may be added.

LENTIL LEMON SOUP

1½ c lentils, washed

7 c water, cold

1 t coriander

3 garlic cloves,
  grated fine

2 T chicken-style
  seasoning
  (See pg. 40)

1 med onion, chopped

Bring to simmer; add:

1 lg potato, unpeeled,
  raw, diced

1½ lbs greens, chopped

Cook 30 minutes. Add:

3 T lemon juice

½ t cumin

Serve topped with thin lemon slices.

MINESTRONE

Cook until macaroni is done.

3 c water

1 c onion, chopped

¾ c celery, chopped

2 c tomatoes, chopped

2 sm zucchini, sliced

1 carrot, coarse grated

¼ t thyme

¼ t savory

½ t garlic powder

1 c whole wheat
  macaroni

Add 2 cups cooked garbanzos, 1 quart of water and chicken-style seasoning (See pg. 40) to taste.

MUSHROOM SOUP

Saute 15 minutes in a small amount of water

1 c onions, chopped

2 c mushrooms, fresh, diced

Add:

1 c water

1 t chicken-style seasoning (See pg. 40)

Blend this until very smooth. Cook until the potatoes are done:

3 c potatoes, raw, finely diced

4 c water

3 c mushrooms, fresh, sliced

1 T chicken-style seasoning (See pg. 40)

Combine both above mixtures and add ¼ teaspoon paprika, ¼ cup dried parsley or ½ cup fresh parsley. Blend and add:

1½ c hot water

1 c cashews

Simmer (do not boil) and serve.

MUSHROOM-PEA SAUCE
(For Pasta or Grain)

Cook until onions are limp:

4 lg onions, sliced

¼ c water

Add:

1 c mushrooms, sliced

1 garlic clove, minced

Cook until mushrooms are tender. Just before serving, add 2 packages (20 ounces) frozen peas. Heat and serve.

PARSNIP SOUP

Cook 15 minutes until parsnips are soft and then blend:

2 lbs parsnips, peeled and thinly sliced

1 lg onion, diced

3 c water

2 T chicken-style seasoning (See pg. 40)

Blend. Then add:

1 c cashews, raw

1 c water, hot

Combine, heat, and serve.

POTATO SOUP

Saute:

1 lg onion, chopped	**¼ c water**

Add:

3 c water	**½ t dill seed**
10 oz vegetables, mixed, frozen(1 pkg.)	**2 T chicken-style seasoning (See pg. 40)**
3 potatoes, unpeeled, diced	

Simmer 25 minutes. Add:

2 c nut cream	**½ t garlic salt**

Heat and serve.

RICE SOUP

Heat to boiling:

6 c water	**3 T chicken-style seasoning (See pg. 40)**

Add:

½ c onion, chopped	**½ c carrot, chopped**
1 c celery, chopped	**1 c brown rice, raw**

Simmer until rice is done, about 45 minutes.

SPINACH SOUP

Serve over rice or millet or spaghetti.

1 c water	**1 t celery seed**
2 med onions, chopped	**½ t garlic salt**
1 t oregano	

Cook until done. Add 2 packages frozen chopped spinach or other greens, or equal amount fresh greens. Cook briefly, only until hot.

TOMATO-RICE OR BARLEY SOUP

Cook until done:

6 c tomato juice	**1½ c onions, diced**
2 c celery, diced	**1 t celery salt**

Add 2½ cups cooked brown rice or barley.

TOMATO SOUP

Heat to boiling:

**24 oz tomato juice
(6 oz. cans)**

1 t celery seed

¼ t cumin

½ t sweet basil

¼ c lemon juice

¼ c parsley

¼ c onion, diced or grated

1 T soy sauce

For cream of tomato, remove from heat and add cashew cream, made by blending 2 cups hot water and 1 cup raw cashews until smooth.

TOMATO STEW

Cook until tender:

6 med potatoes, cubed   **1 c onions, diced**

Add and heat only, 2½ cups fresh or canned chopped tomatoes. Salt, if needed.

VEGETABLE BISQUE

Cook until tender:

1½ c carrots, diced

2 c leeks or onions, sliced

2 c potatoes, raw, diced

3½ c water

**2 T chicken-style seasoning
(See pg. 40)**

Add 1 cup watercress. Cook 2 minutes. Blend ingredients and add 1 cup cashew milk. Serve cold with thinly sliced raw green onions and croutons.

VEGETABLE SOUP (3 Ways)

Cook until tender:

4 onions, coarse chopped

4 carrots, sliced

4 celery stalks with leaves, sliced

2 c green beans

4 parsnips, sliced thinly

1 c parsley, chopped

½ t thyme

½ t basil

salt if needed

3 qts water

A. Drain for broth.

B. Eat as Is.

C. Blend.

Tofu Dishes

TOFU

Be sure the tofu is fresh and drain several hours before using.

COOL SLAW

Combine:

1 c carrots, grated	**⅔ c sunflower seeds**
2 c cabbage, shredded	**1 c celery, diced**
½ c peanuts, chopped	

Dressing:

Blend.

1 c tofu	**8 dates**
¼ c lemon juice	**¼ c water**

FONDU SAUCE FOR VEGETABLES

2 c water	**½ c cashews, raw**
1 lg potato	**¼ c flaked yeast**
1 carrot	**2 t paprika**
1 onion	**½ c lemon juice**
1 tofu brick (1 lb.)	**2½ t salt**
pinch garlic powder	

Use 1 cup water to cook vegetables (cut fine). Add 1 cup water, lemon juice, cashews, blend. Then add seasonings to the vegetables. Last, add tofu, blending well. Makes about 7 cups.

TOFU LASAGNA

Tomato Sauce:

½ c onion, chopped	**1 garlic clove, minced**
½ c celery, chopped	**½ t oregano**
¼ c green pepper, chopped	**½ t sweet basil**
	½ t salt
½ c carrots, shredded	**1 qt tomatoes, blended**

Combine ingredients for sauce and simmer 1 hour. Cook lasagna noodles until tender. Drain 1 block tofu by crumbling into colander. Mix tofu with the following cashew cheese:

Cashew Cheese:

1 c water

1 c cashews, raw

3 T Brewer's yeast

½ t onion

½ garlic salt

1 t salt

¼ c lemon juice

1 jar pimentos (sm),
  or some canned
  tomato for color

Liquefy all. In large oblong Pyrex dish, layer noodles, sauce and then tofu cheese mixture. Repeat, using 3 layers of noodles. Drizzle top with some reserved cashew cheese. Bake.

TOFU MAYONNAISE

May be used as sauce on baked potato, green salad or on bread.

1 (lb.) tofu

2 c garbanzos,
  cooked

½ c cashews

2 t salt

2 T lemon juice

½ c sesame seeds

Add liquid from garbanzos and enough water to equal 2 cups and 1 clove garlic. Blend.

TOFU AND MUSHROOMS

Blend and cook until thickened.

1 c water, hot

¼ c soy sauce

10 dates

1½ T cornstarch

Simmer 8 minutes.

2 c mushrooms

1 c green onions,
  chopped

1 lb tofu, drained and
  cut in 1 inch cubes

½ c water

Add sauce and serve.

TOFU PATTIES

1½ c garbanzos, mashed

1 lb tofu, crumbled

2 c bread crumbs,
  fresh, diced

Blend and add:

1 med onion

¼ c water

1½ c olives

2 T chicken-style
  seasoning
  (See pg. 40)

Mix well and drop by spoonfuls on Pam-sprayed cookie sheets. Bake for 1 hour at 300°.

PEANUT TOFU

Blend:

½ c peanut butter	½ c water
¼ c lemon juice	10 dates

Pour over:

2 c pineapple chunks	1 c peanuts, chopped
1 c water chestnuts, sliced	2 bananas, sliced
1 lb tofu, cut in cubes	

SALAD

Combine:

2 cucumbers, quartered and sliced in ½ inch chunks	1 sm onion, diced

Blend and use as a dressing:

¼ c water	¼ t cumin
¼ c lemon juice	½ t salt
½ c tofu	6 dates

TOFU SMOOTHIE DRINK

Blend:

6 oz tofu (soft)	1 c strawberries
1 c apple juice	6 dates
2 bananas	1 t vanilla

TOFU (SOUR) SOUP

4 c water	2 T lemon juice
1 T chicken-style seasoning (See pg. 40)	4 oz tomato sauce
	1 T soy sauce

Bring above ingredients to a boil then add:

½ lb tofu, crumbled	½ c water chestnuts, sliced
1 c mushrooms, canned, sliced (opt)	2 c brown rice, cooked

Bring to boil and add:

2 T cornstarch	3 T water, cold

Serve topped with finely diced scallions or chives.

TOFU (Homemade)

Blend:

4 c	**water**	**½ c**	**whole wheat flour**
2¼ c	**soy flour**	**⅓ c**	**lemon juice**
⅔ c	**pimentos**	**½ t**	**garlic salt**
1 T	**salt**	**1 T**	**food yeast**

Pour in a loaf pan and bake 2 hours at 275°. Turn off oven heat, but keep tofu in oven 1 more hour. Slice or crumble or cube for serving.

Write an extra recipe here:

Vegetables

ACORN SQUASH

Fill cavity with bread dressing. Wrap in foil. Bake for 1 hour at 350°.

ASPARAGUS

Boiling tied in bunches, stalks down, saves mangling the tops. Good served hot or cold. May use Golden Sauce.

BROCCOLI

Watch carefully to keep bright color. Do not over cook. Using flat pan, as electric skillet, means one layer, little water and broccoli cooks in less than 5 minutes. Lift cover often to keep color.

BRUSSELS SPROUTS AND CORN

Combine and cook Brussels sprouts, whole kernel corn, sliced water chestnuts or mushrooms in salted water.

BEETS

Cook tiny beets, tops and all. Small beets need only a little salt, or add a little fresh lemon juice, if you wish.

BLENDER BORSCH

Blend well:

1 c cashew cream	slice lemon (1 inch) with peel
2 c beets, diced	
salt	½ sm onion

Just before serving, add 1 cup chopped ice. Blend briefly and serve at once.

PICKLED BEETS

2 t lemon juice	1 t salt
2 c apple juice or pineapple juice	

Heat to boiling point and pour over 1 quart cooked beets. Let stand 48 hours. Liquid can be used more than once, or can be thickened for hot beets.

BEETS PIQUANT

Cook 1½ cups grated beets in water with juice of 2 oranges, grated peel of 1 orange, ½ teaspoons vega salt, juice of 1 lemon and ½ teaspoon cardamom. When done, thicken with cornstarch.

CAULIFLOWER AND TOMATOES

Combine and cook cauliflower flowerettes, sliced zucchini and quartered tomatoes in small amount of water.

CAULIFLOWER AND DIP

Eat it raw or cook briefly; add Avocado Dip.

CREAM OF CAULIFLOWER

Cook and mash 1 head cauliflower, 3 medium potatoes, add salt, ¼ cup chopped parsley and ½ cup nut cream.

CABBAGE

Delicious raw. Cook briefly with poppy seeds, vega salt, and add ripe olives (chopped).

CABBAGE AND CORN

Combine and cook shredded cabbage and whole kernel corn in a small amount salted water.

CABBAGE AND VEGETABLES

Combine and cook green beans, onion rings, shredded cabbage and thinly sliced carrots in a small amount of salted water.

CABBAGE IN CREAM

Cook 2 pounds sliced cabbage in 1 cup water. Combine and add:

1 T cornstarch	**½ c nut cream***
4 T lemon juice	**salt and caraway seeds, as desired**

Heat briefly to thicken.

*Nut cream is made by whizzing 1 cup water and ½ cup raw nuts in blender until smooth.

RED CABBAGE

Cook until done:

2 lbs red cabbage, sliced

1 c water

salt (it helps the cabbage to keep its color)

Combine and add and cook to thicken:

1 T cornstarch

2 T lemon juice

CABBAGE ROLLS

20 cabbage leaves, cooked until tender,

or 1 head cabbage, sliced thin

Combine and cook briefly:

1 c navy beans, cooked

1 c onions, finely diced

1 c rice, cooked

1 c tomatoes, chopped

¼ c parsley

½ c celery, chopped

¼ c green pepper, chopped

1 t savory salt

Put a large spoonful in a cabbage leaf; roll up; place closely in cabbage leaf-lined baking pan. Heat 15 to 20 minutes at 350°. Or cook sauce until nearly done. Add shredded cabbage on top and cook no more than 8 to 10 minutes.

CABBAGE SOUP

Cook until done:

1 c onion, diced

3 med potatoes, cubed

6 c water

vegesalt to taste

½ t dill seed

½ t poppy seed

½ t celery seed

Add a few minutes before serving, 1 small head thinly sliced cabbage and 1 cup chopped parsley.

EGGPLANT

Cook in a little salted water for 15 minutes then drain:

2 lg eggplants, peeled, cubed,
Cook 45 minutes:

1 c onion, diced

½ c parsley, chopped

1 c brown rice, raw

2 c water

Combine all ingredients plus 1 teaspoon Italian herbs and 1 cup bread crumbs. Two cups tomatoes, quartered. Bake for 30 minutes at 350°.

EGGPLANT BAKED

Peel and dice and cook in ½ cup salted water, 1 medium eggplant. Drain well. Add:

1½ c bread crumbs, soft

¼ t marjoram

½ c nut milk

½ c parsley, snipped

Bake at 350° for 30 minutes.

EGGPLANT BROILED

Brown slices of eggplant under the broiler. Put in a casserole and top with sliced green onions, garlic powder, tomato slices, lemon juice, sweet basil. Bake 40 minutes at 350°.

EGGPLANT CASSEROLE NUMBER 1

Peel and chop one large eggplant. Add:

1 c onion, finely diced

2 c tomato juice

1½ c millet or brown rice, cooked

1 t cumin

1 t chicken-style seasoning (See pg. 40)

¼ c parsley, snipped

1 c whole kernel corn

Bake at 350° for 45 minutes.

EGGPLANT CASSEROLE NUMBER 2

1 lg eggplant (about 1½ lbs.)

⅓ c water

1 med onion, chopped

¼ lb mushrooms, sliced

salt to taste

1 garlic clove, minced or pressed

15 oz tomato sauce (1 lg can)

½ t dry basil

½ t oregano leaves

Cut eggplant into ½ inch thick slices; arrange in a single layer on a rimmed baking sheet. Bake, uncovered, in a 450° oven until browned and very soft, about 30 minutes.

Heat ⅓ cup water in a frying pan over medium heat; add onion, mushrooms, and garlic and cook until soft. Add tomato sauce, basil, and oregano; simmer, uncovered, for 10 minutes. Season to taste with salt.

Layer about half the eggplant in a shallow 1½ quart casserole; top with half the sauce. Repeat layers. Bake, uncovered, in a 350° oven, until hot and bubbly, about 25 minutes.

EGGPLANT CASSEROLE NUMBER 3

Cut 2 eggplants in ½ inch slices. Place on a cookie sheet and bake at 400° for 30 minutes. Turn after 15 minutes. Blend:

1½ c **tomato juice**	¼ c **parsley**
1 sm onion	**1 celery rib**

Layer in a casserole the eggplant, the tomato mixture, bread crumbs and ground peanuts. Bake for 20 minutes at 350°.

EGGPLANT STUFFED

Cook 2 whole eggplants for 20 minutes in boiling water. Cool, drain, cut in half lengthwise, scoop out the pulp.

Filling:

all the chopped pulp	¼ c **parsley, chopped**
½ c **onion, finely diced**	¼ c **celery and leaves,**
1 **tomatoes, diced**	**chopped**
⅔ c **brown rice, cooked**	½ t **garlic salt**

Mix and fill eggplants. Bake for 15 minutes at 400 degrees.

GREENS

A. Cook 1 pound shredded spinach in 2 tablespoons soy sauce and ¼ cup water.

B. Cook 1 pound chopped spinach, 1 cup cooked brown rice, 2 tablespoons finely chopped onion, ¼ teaspoon thyme and ¾ cup nut milk.

C. Swiss Chard. This is a mild flavor green. Chop and cook only to wilt. Serve at once with sauce for greens.

GREEN CASSEROLE

Blend:

**3 c spinach or other
greens, wilted**

Set aside. Blend:

**1½ c any legume,
cooked**

1 T beef-style seasoning

1½ c water

Combine greens and beans. Add:

**2 c whole wheat bread
crumbs, fresh**

Bake at 350° for ½ hour.

GREEN PEAS

Cook peas only a few minutes In water, ½ teaspoon onion salt, ⅛ teaspoon garlic salt and ¼ teaspoon marjoram. Tiny cooked onions can be added.

GREEN PEAS AND MINT

Serve peas with fresh snipped mint or dried mint and grated orange or lemon peel.

PEAS AND WHEAT

**½ c whole kernel wheat,
cooked**

**1 pkg peas, frozen
(or most any other
vegetable)**

Serve hot.

GREEN PEA SOUP

Blend until smooth:

2 c hot water

1 c cashews, raw

1 T onion powder

¼ t celery seed

1 t salt

dash garlic and thyme

Add and blend 1 pound fresh or frozen peas, 3 cups hot water. Heat, but do not boil; serve.

GREEN BEANS

A. Add very finely chopped raw onion and hot lemon juice just before serving.

B. Add water chestnuts or mushrooms.

C. Put small amount of Italian herbs in cooking water of fresh beans.

D. Cook beans; add quartered tomatoes and sliced zucchini and cook 8 minutes.

E. Add summer savory and parsley for flavor or thin onion rings are good, too.

GREEN BEANS CALIFORNIA

1 lg onion, sliced	½ t thyme
1 qt green beans, fresh	¼ t oregano
½ c water	¼ t summer savory
1 t vege salt	¼ t marjoram

Cooking time varies as to the maturity of the beans.

GREEN BEANS AND SEEDS

Cook:

1 lb green beans	½ t basil
½ c water	1 t vege salt
1 onion, thinly sliced	¼ c sunflower seeds

MUSHROOMS

Cook large fresh whole mushrooms slowly in small amounts—1 part soy sauce and 2 parts water—on griddle or fry pan.

MUSHROOM ROAST

1 c celery	1 can water chestnuts
1 lb mushrooms, fresh	1 c cashew milk
1 c onions, chopped	1 c cashew nuts
1 can mushrooms	2 c brown rice, cooked

Chop onions, celery, and mushrooms. Cook these three together in small amount of water until tender. Add all other ingredients. Bake for 40 minutes at 300°.

ONIONS AND BEANS

Put whole small onions in baked beans before baking.

ONIONS BAKED

Bake small onions, small carrots and 1 inch slant cut celery. Add vege salt.

ONIONS BAKED WITH RICE

Peel 6 to 8 onions, slice crosswise, and steam until tender. Layer in baking dish with 2 cups cooked rice. Pour over contents—2 cups cashew milk seasoned with 1 teaspoon vegesalt. Put thin green pepper slices or whole green beans or green limas on top. Bake at 350° for 20 minutes.

ONIONS BOILED

Cook onion halves (cut side up) in one layer in fry pan with water nearly to cover and a sprinkle of salt. Simmer about 30 minutes until done. Drain well and carefully. Serve with paprika, chopped almond and snipped parsley.

ONIONS CREAMED

Cook together and then blend 2 pounds cubed potatoes and 2 pounds onions. Add:

1 T tomato puree	salt
1 T lemon juice	½ c nut cream

Mix together.

POTATOES

Baked, boiled in jackets, riced or (?) potatoes with:

A. Paprika and parsley

B. Onion and garlic salt

C. Finely chopped green onion and grated lemon peel.

D. Hot cashew cream seasoned with chicken-style seasoning (See pg. 40) and onion powder

POTATO BAKE

Slice thinly 6 medium size unpeeled potatoes. Cover with water; let set 30 minutes. Drain.

Prepare casserole by spraying with Pam. Coat sides and bottom with dry crumbs. Layer potato slices and thinly sliced onions and salt. Top with a few crumbs. Bake for 90 minutes at 350 degrees, covered; unmold.

POTATO CAKES

1 c onion, finely chopped	½ c water
3 c potatoes, cooked, mashed or diced	½ t garlic powder
	1 t onion powder
3 c bread crumbs	salt as needed

Mix well and spread thin on cookie sheet or as patties. Bake at 350° until crisp.

POTATOES WITH TOMATO

Cook 3 pounds of potatoes. Mash the potatoes with 2 cups nut milk and onion salt and 3 tablespoons tomato puree. Serve.

POTATOES MASHED OR DICED

Add mashed carrots or rutabagas or finely shredded cabbage or spinach or corn, peas, chopped onion or blended fresh limas.

POTATO PATTIES

Cook 6 medium size cubed potatoes or equal amount of rice with 1 cup diced onion. Drain and partially mash. Add:

1½ corn, drained	¼ t garlic powder
¼ c parsley, chopped	½ t onion powder
½ c bread crumbs	1 t vege salt

Form patties or spread thinly on cookie sheet. Bake until brown and crisp.

POTATO SOUP (Cold Vichyssoise)

Cook:

1 c onions, chopped	3 T chicken-style seasoning (See pg. 40)
4 c potatoes, sliced	
4 c water	

Add 1¼ cups nut cream (½ cup raw cashews to 1 cup hot water). Blend all until creamy and refrigerate several hours. Serve cold.

POTATO SOUP

Heat:

5 med potatoes, cooked, diced	**1 T chicken-style seasoning (See pg. 40)**
2 c water	**½ t garlic salt**

Blend until smooth:

1 T onion, dried	**1 c cashews, raw**
2 c water, hot	**½ t celery seed**

Combine and heat and serve.

POTATOES STEWED

Cook until done:

1 lg onion, coarsely chopped	**2½ c water**
	½ t garlic salt
6 med potatoes, cut in inch slices	**¼ t thyme**
	1 bay leaf (discard after cooking)

Add ½ cup chopped parsley after draining. Serve.

SWEET POTATOES OR YAMS

A. Mash sweet potatoes. Top with thin orange slices and bake.

B. Layer 1 inch slices cooked sweet potatoes in a baking dish. Heat in saucepan 2 cups orange juice, 1 cup light or dark raisins and 2 tablespoons cornstarch. Cook to thicken. Remove from heat; add ½ cup walnuts and pour over potatoes. Heat, covered at 350° for about 20 to 25 minutes.

C. Serve sweet potatoes or yams with hot applesauce.

POTATOES—SWEET OR YAMS

Lay 1 inch thick cooked yam slices and 1 inch raw apple slices, lightly salted, in casserole. Add crushed pineapple with juice. Cover and cook until apples are done at 350°.

SWEET POTATO FLUFF

3 med yams or sweet
    potatoes, cooked
    and mashed

8 oz pineapple, canned,
    crushed

½ c water chestnuts,
    sliced

½ t salt

Put in shallow baking dish topped with dry bread crumbs. Bake at 350°
for 40 minutes.

SWEET POTATOES OR YAMS

Cook, skin and slice 6 medium size yams or sweet potatoes. Combine
in pan and cook until thickened:

1 c orange juice

grated rind from
    1 orange

1 T cornstarch

Pour sauce over yams in casserole. Bake at 350° for 45 minutes.

SAUERKRAUT STEW

1½ c sauerkraut

3 c. tomato juice,
    unsalted

1 t caraway or dill seed

6 med potatoes, cut in 1
    inch chunks

Cook until potatoes are done and serve.

SAUERKRAUT STUFFING

Mix well:

2 c onions, chopped,
    sauteed in ½ c
    water

2 lbs sauerkraut

3 potatoes, cooked,
    grated

1 t dill seed

2 bread slices,
    crumbled

Fill large, halved, seeded, but not peeled, zucchini squash. Cook 45
minutes at 325°,

TOMATOES

Dip tomato slices in seasoned bread crumbs and parsley and broil.

TOMATO-CASHEW SOUP

Combine 3 cups tomato juice or blended canned tomatoes with:

**1 c cashews, raw,
    ground fine**

1 t onion powder

¼ t garlic powder

**1 bay leaf (discard
    when cooked)**

Heat well and serve.

TOMATO-CORN SOUP

Wash and core 3 pounds fresh tomatoes, chop. Cook in 1 pint of water for 10 minutes.

Cut kernels from 2 ears fresh corn and add ½ cup water, 1 bay leaf (discard after cooked), 1 pinch thyme, ¼ teaspoon marjoram, ¼ teaspoon basil, 1 tablespoon chicken-style seasoning (See pg. 40). Cook 7 minutes. Put tomatoes through sieve and add to corn. Simmer 10 minutes and serve.

TOMATO SOUP

Heat to boiling:

**46 oz tomato juice,
     canned**

1 t celery seed

¼ c lemon juice

¼ t cumin

½ t sweet basil

¼ c parsley

¼ c onion, dried or grated

1 T soy sauce

For cream of tomato, add cashew cream; blend until smooth 2 cups hot water and 1 cup raw cashews.

TOMATO STEW

Cook:

6 med potatoes, cubed

2 c water

1 c onions

Add 2½ cups fresh or canned tomatoes, chopped.

TOMATO WHEAT

Combine cooked coarse cracked wheat, onion, tomato and parsley. Serve hot or cold.

VITAMIN SOUP

Cook together until tender:

½ c cabbage	1 c sweet potato
½ c carrots	½ c onion
1 c potatoes	½ c celery
½ c string beans	2 c water

Add ½ cup tomatoes and salt. Blend 10 seconds. Add 1 cup cooked barley. Heat and serve.

VEGETABLE COMBINATION

Combine and cook briefly:

1½ c carrots, diagonally sliced	1 c mushrooms, sliced (opt)
1½ c cauliflower, sliced	1 c green limas
6 green onions, sliced	1½ c water
	3 T soy sauce

Add 1 can whole green beans. May be slightly thickened. Heat only; serve at once. Add almonds, if desired.

VEGETABLE GRAVY CASSEROLE

Layer in a casserole dish slices of cooked potatoes, slices of fresh tomatoes, whole cooked green beans, thinly sliced raw cabbage. Add thinly sliced raw onions. Pour over all a cashew gravy. Bake at 350° for 45 minutes.

ZUCCHINI

A. Very small zucchini are always best. Do not peel. Slice in half lengthwise. Sprinkle with herb salt. Use a mixture of onion, garlic and celery. Cook in small amount of water until barely done. They are delicious.

B. Cook coarsely grated zucchini, 1½ cups whole kernel corn with liquid, 1 small thinly sliced onion, and 2 large tomatoes, cut in wedges. Sprinkle with 1 teaspoon dill seed or 1 tablespoon freshly snipped dill.

C. Eat zucchini raw, too.

VEGETABLES MEXICAN

Cook 10 minutes:

½ c water

1 c celery, finely sliced

1 c onion, chopped

Add and cook 5 minutes:

2 c corn, canned, with liquid

Add and just heat:

2 c tomatoes, fresh or
    canned

1 t chicken-style
    seasoning
    (See pg. 40)

1 c mushrooms, fresh or
    canned, sliced (opt)

1 t cumin

VEGETABLES ON PASTA

Crisp cook:

1 c mushrooms, sliced
    (opt)

1 c cauliflower, sliced

1 c green peas

1 c carrots, sliced

1 c zucchini, sliced

1 c water

Blend:

1½ c water, hot

1 t chicken-style
    seasoning (See pg. 40)

½ c cashews, raw

Add nut milk to the vegetables and serve over pasta or brown rice or barley.

ZUCCHINI CAULIFLOWER

Cook zucchini in 1 inch slices; cauliflower broken into small flowerettes. Top with Avocado Dressing.

ZUCCHINI HERB CASSEROLE

Cook 7 minutes:

5 c zucchini, cubed

1 c green onions, sliced

1 garlic clove, minced

¼ c water

Add:

2 tomatoes, peeled and
    chopped

1 c brown rice, cooked

½ t basil

½ t paprika

½ t oregano

Bake for 25 to 35 minutes in a 350° oven.

Write your extra recipes here:

About Vitamins

Vitamin B_1 (thiamine) aids in the release of energy from carbohydrates and helps in the synthesis of a nervous-system chemical. Found in lima beans, okra, onions, potatoes.

Vitamin B_2 (riboflavin) helps release energy from carbohydrates, proteins & fats, and helps in the maintenance of mucous membranes. Found in dried beans and peas, broccoli, collards, mushrooms, okra, winter squash.

Vitamin B_3 (niacin) works with B_1 and B_2 in producing energy in cells. Found in dried peas and beans, mushrooms, potatoes.

Vitamin C helps maintain capillaries, bones and teeth. Found in sweet peppers, potatoes, Brussels sprouts, tomatoes, broccoli, collards.

Vitamin E aids in the formation of red blood cells and muscle tissue and protects the body's source of vitamin A and C. Found in spinach, asparagus, broccoli leaves.

Calcium builds bones and teeth, helps maintain bone strength, aids in muscle contraction and blood clotting. Found in broccoli, collards, dandelion greens.

Potassium aids muscle contraction, transmission of nerve impulses and the release of energy from carbohydrates, proteins and fats. Found in potatoes, squash, dried peas and beans.

Iron keeps red blood cells healthy. Found in lima beans, broccoli, spinach, potatoes.

Do You Need a B12 Supplement?

by Milton Crane, M.D.   NEWSTART Research Director
Used by permission.

Total vegetarians (vegans) are generally active and energetic. They have no obvious symptoms of B12 deficiency, and yet many are concerned about getting enough B12. Why is there confusion about the need for this vitamin? There are several reasons. First, early methods of assaying B12 in foods indicated that a measurable amount was present in several foods. However, both the early microorganism method and later on the initial radio immuno-assay method were not selective enough. Researchers were not able to discriminate between an ineffective corrinoid chemical and the active B12 corrinoid. Second, many vegetarians desire to use only natural means for their health, not something in a pill.

It is now generally agreed that the only source of biologically active B12 for humans is a residue of bacterial growth which is not made by plants or animals. B12 is an animal product resulting from bacterial growth in meat, fish or fowl. It occurs in milk as a result of the growth in bacteria in the ruminant stomach of the cow and from bacterial growth in the milk.

For good health's sake, cleanliness demands that people avoid eating germs and their residues. Consequently, if one puts the totally vegetarian Egyptian fruit bats in captivity on a daily diet of fresh water and wash or peeled fruit, they become B12 deficient; half of them in the first eighty days. (It's ironic that eating unwashed fruits and vegetables could provide much of the needed B12 if mankind were not afraid of harmful bacteria.)

It is necessary for the body to identify and absorb active B12 if it is in food. First, B12 must be combined with an "R-binder" in the stomach. This complex R-binder with B12 moves from the stomach into the first portion of the small intestines (duodenam), where the intestinal enzymes exchange intrinsic factor, (made by the stomach) for the R-binder. Intrinsic factor combines only with potent B12; it protects it and enables the wall of the last eight feet of the small intestines to absorb it.

If there is not enough B12 in the food or if the B12 isn't bound by the R-binder or if the stomach does not make enough intrinsic factor or if the intrinsic factor is not united with the B12, then the liver and tissue stores of B12 begin to be depleted, and the person gradually becomes deficient in B12. The several chemical processes that are dependent on B12 slow down or cease to work. As a result, the bone marrow begins to put out slightly larger immature red blood cells and immature white blood cells, and the immune system suffers. Also, the cells which line the intestinal tract and the nerve tissue become defective.

Research was done at Weimar Institute on 95 adults (including college students) and nine children (ages three to nine years) who for twelve months or longer had been on a total vegetarian (vegan) diet (except for possibly a church potluck once a month). Nine children and ten adults who were on the same vegan diet, yet when habitually used a commercial powdered soy milk which was fortified with vitamin B12, served as controls. Serum B12 and MCV (mean corpuscular volume or average red cell size) were measured by a commercial clinical laboratory.

A brief summary of the findings follows: The average serum B12 dropped 34.5% in college students two months after starting the vegan diet and declined slightly more five months starting the total vegetarian diet. Fifty-two percent of volunteers on the total vegetarian diet for a year or more had serum B12 levels below the 200 pg/ml, 31% were between 200 and 299 pg/ml, and 71% were 300 or above. The average MCV of all those in the total vegetarian diet for a year or more was significantly larger ($p=0.01$) than that of the controls on the vitamin B12 fortified soy milk. Only one of the 39 persons with a B12 level below 200 pg/ml failed to respond promptly to the oral administration of a readily soluble vitamin B12 preparation. If the vitamin B12 tablet was to firm, the B12 was not absorbed unless it was crushed (chewed) before swallowing. Allen and associates report that vitamin B12 is changed to an inactive analog of B12 while in a vitamin-mineral capsule which contain iron and copper.

Weimar researchers conclude that all persons who go on a total vegetarian diet should regularly take about 50 mcg daily or 500 mg once a week as a supplement of B12 in a form that can be readily absorbed or chewed by mouth.

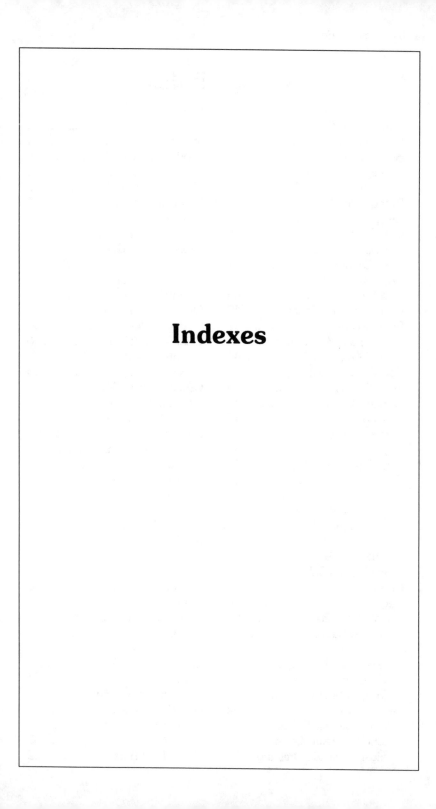

Indexes

Recipe Index

Alphabetical Index

Gluten Free Index

Other books by TEACH Services, Inc.

Activated Charcoal *David Cooney*..............................$ 7.95
This publication represents an attempt to gather together most of what has been reported to date on the use of activated charcoal as an oral antidote and as a remedy for other ailments.

Adam's Table *Reggi Burnett*..$ 8.95
A cookbook to help the user obtain optimum healthier and happier lifestyle through changes in their cooking style. Originated from Adam's Table Restaurant in Albuquerque, NM.

American Democracy *R. S. McClanahan*.....................$18.95
Will its maintenance be a 21st century reality? An overview of an evolving Constitutional "Achilles' Heel".

An Adventure in Cooking *Joanne Nowack*.................$12.95
This book has been compiled especially to teach young people, in a step-by-step, progressive way, the art of vegetarian cookery. Cooking is a real art, and very practical one too, since we need to eat every day.

Angel At My Side *Bob Hoyt* ....$ 8.95
The author, a pastor, Bible worker, and Literature evangelists, tells of his experiences with angels, dogs, guns, horses, floods, skunks, life threatening hazards, and a heart-wrenching deathbed vigil.

The Antichrist 666 *William Josiah Sutton* ....$ 8.95
Positive proof for Bible Believing People: Who the beast is; Who his image is; What the mark of the beast is; How to count the number of the beast. Edited by Roy Allan Anderson, D.D.

The Anti-Christ Exposed *Dan Jarrard* ....$ 5.95
A biblical and historical study of the counterfeit religious system which is against God and His people.

The Art of Massage *J. H. Kellogg*.................................$12.95
A practical manual for the student, the nurse and the practitioner.

Aunt Joanne's Plays *Joanne Johnson*.........................$ 9.95
This collection gives alternative Christmas themes to work with rather than just the regular Joseph and Mary or Wise Men themes.

Aunt Joanne's Skits *Joanne Johnson* ....$ 9.95
A collection of skits that children can act out, training them to not only hear, but see the results of Biblical morals.

Caring Kitchen Recipes *Gloria Lawson* $12.95
Specializes in recipes for better health that features: whole grains, vegetarian, dairy-free and nourishing dessert recipes.

The Celtic Church in Britain *Leslie Hardinge* ....$ 8.95
This is an authoritative study of the beliefs and practice of the Celtic Church which at the same time holds much interest for the non-specialist, containing as it does fascinating descriptions of the life of the early Celtic Christians in their monastic walled villages modelled on the Old Testament cities of refuge. Their elaborate penitential discipline was based on Old Testament compensatory regulations. Obedience to the Scriptures led them to establish a remarkable theocracy based on the laws of the Pentateuch and including the keeping of the Seventh-day Sabbath.

Children's Bible Lessons *Bessie White* ....$ 3.95
These seven Children's Bible Lessons are prepared for use during Evangelistic Meetings, Bible seminars, Vacation Bible Schools, or at the Church's discretion.

Christian Apparel *Allen & Patti Barnes* ....$ 4.95
This book is an appeal to Seventh-day Adventist to establish a new standard—not the customs of society or of the church, but the words of Scripture, and the every specific instructions which God has so bountifully given through the Spirit of Prophecy.

Convert's Catechism *Peter Geiermann*........................$ 2.50
The quoted statement on changing solemnity from Saturday to Sunday can be found in this reproduction.

Divine Philosophy & Science *G. Paulien* $19.95
All of the principles of the Bible and the Spirit of Prophecy are designed to allow us to function in perfect harmony with God Himself. This book discusses the methods and means of healthful living. It deals with going back to First Things, and relying by faith upon the substances which God has established for our benefit.

Don't Drink Your Milk *Frank Oski, MD* ....$ 7.95
Dr. Oski, the head of Pediatrics at Johns Hopkins University School of Medicine, gives the frightening new medical facts about the world's most overrated nutrient.

Earthly Life of Jesus *Ken LeBrun* $19.95
Biblical accounts of each event in Christ's earthly life carefully arranged together from the KJV Bible. Words of Jesus in red with full index.

The Elijah People *Ken LeBrun*.....................................$ 1.00
Those who, in the spirit and power of Elijah, take part in this final
work of reform, will be those who, like Elijah, will be taken to
heaven seeing death. Let us be among them.

Fire Bell in the Night *Ralph Moss*.............................$ 5.95
News items and stories from both the secular press and from
religious newspapers, along with journals and articles by secular
and religious authors will be linked with Bible prophecy to reveal
a most startling scenario in just the last few years, and to lay a case
to expose an undreamed of enemy who is rapidly winning the
confidence of most of this world's inhabitants.

From Eden to Eden *J. H. Waggoner*...........................$ 9.95
A most interesting study of the more important historic and pro-
phetic portions of the Scriptures.

God's DNA for Pure Religion *Ernest H. J. Steed*.......$ 5.95
This book presents a key formula to measure truth and error, the
genuine or the counterfeit, so essential in today's world of confusion.

God's Justice—Administered in Love *D. Beman*.....$ 5.95
You can learn the secret of how to stand firm in the Judgment, without
being afraid, and yet maintain a healthy, respectful fear of God.

Gospel In Creation *E. J. Waggoner*...........................$ 6.95
This book directs our wandering gaze to the open pages of God's
created works as the expression of the gospel, the power of God
to save from sin. Facsimile Reprint.

Healing By God's Natural Methods *Al. Wolfsen* ......$ 4.95
Al. Wolfsen has taught hundreds of sick people how to use only
simple, non-poisonous remedies.

Healthful Living *Ellen G. White* $10.95
Wherever this book has been received, it has been recognized as
a veritable storehouse of seed thoughts relating to the great
practical themes with which it deals. Facsimile Reprint.

Healthy Food Choices *Leona R. Alderson*...................$14.95
Some special features include: guidelines for menu planning,
breakfast suggestions, ideas for brown bag lunches, and much
more!

Helps to Bible Study *J. L. Shuler*................................$ 2.95
A Bible marking system which contains Bible studies covering
twenty-eight topics including "The Second Coming," "The Seal of
the Living God," "Bible Temperance," and "Christian in Dress."
It is simple and practical in its approach, and will benefit all ages.

Holy Spirit Seminar   *Harold Penninger* ....$ 7.95
A collection of Holy Spirit Seminars for study, inspiration, etc.

Hoofbeats in Time   *W. G. Moore* ....$ 6.95
The title is an allusion to one of the 4 major prophecies of Revelation—*the Four Horsemen of Apocalypse.* These horsemen hold fascinating predictions concerning the world we live in, events both in the past and the future to come.

Hydrotherapy—Simple Treatments   *Thomas/Dail* ....$ 8.95
Help your body overcome common diseases using hydrotherapy and simple home treatments.

The Illuminati 666   *William Josiah Sutton* ....$ 8.95
Find out about the Illuminati, its startling history, and how powerful it has become. Includes a study of the origins of false religions, and the forms they are taking today. Introduction by Roy Allan Anderson, D.D.

In Heavenly Places Now!   *Richard Parent* ....$ 5.95
A devotional study of the sanctuary service which seeks to focus our attention on our High Priest, Jesus Christ, who ever lives to make intercession for us.

Incredible Edibles   *Eriann Hullquist* ....$ 7.95
Some "health" meals taste bland, some are hard to make, others require strange or hard to find ingredients. Eriann has developed a simple method of meal preparation where each recipe looks good and tastes great.

Judgment?? Whose Judgment?   *Robert Frazier* ....$ 6.95
Is God really on trial and being judged? This book explores this question and others.

The Justified Walk   *Frank Phillips* ....$ 8.95
Before you can rightly tackle a problem, you must first be able to clearly understand its nature. Before you can discuss it with others, you must first define your terms. In this book Elder Phillips makes clear how the plan of salvation works in our daily lives. Faith, Grace, Sin, Justification, Sanctification and Righteousness are made real and tangible.

Lessons On Faith   *Jones & Waggoner* ....$ 6.95
This is a compilation of articles and sermons given in the 1890's by Jones and Waggoner on Righteousness By Faith.

Let the Holy Spirit Speak   *Garrie Fraser Williams* ......$ 4.95
A remarkable new book that is not just a study guide but a unique resource of Bible study methods and small group information.

Miracles At The Door   *Don Draper*..............................$ 8.95
Reading this will encourage the reader and show them how God still works miracles even in this modern world we live in.

Mystical Medicine   *Warren Peters*................................$ 7.95
Many people today have come to believe that our modern, technological system of health care in the Western world isn't proving to be the great boon that it was once thought to be. Frustrated and disillusioned people are turning to "more natural" methods of treatment. As we become aware of the intimate connection between the physical, mental and spiritual aspects of our nature, we are flocking to holistic medicine by the thousands.

Living Fountains/Broken Cisterns   *Sutherland*..........$12.95
This book tells how we should set up our education systems to follow the heavenly blueprint. The goal is to have the best Christian schools in the world.

Nature's Banquet   *Living Springs*................................$12.95
Cooking is an Art and a Science. You will find that the art and science of cooking is especially enjoyable when using natural foods and when learning to be a vegetarian cook. The art of food preparation will give you the opportunity to exercise your enlightened preference and your personality to create attractive, delicious and nutritious meals. The science of cooking involves techniques and properties of food which affect its successful preparation.

Nutrition Workshop Guide   *E. Hullquist* .... 10 for $ 9.95
Chock full of nutritional recipes, as well as lots of helpful nutritional tips for special situations, such as road trips, fast foods, etc.

Pioneer Stories   *Arthur W. Spalding*..............................$ 9.95
It is good for children to know what their fathers and mothers did; for sometimes that makes a pattern of what the children should do. Especially is this true if the children are set to finish the work their parents began. And that is the reason why this book is written, to tell the children of the pioneers in the second advent movement the beginnings of that movement, and reasons why they are to carry it on.

Place of Herbs in Rational Therapy   *D. E. Robinson*...$ .90
Quotations relative to the use of herbs in therapy from D. E. Robinson, who was the secretary to Mrs. White.

Power of Prayer   *E. G. White* ....$ 7.95
Prayer is our connection with God—our strength, our bridge to heaven! As we pray, the Holy Spirit Himself unites in our petitions

and "maketh intercession for us." We are not alone in our battle of life; all heaven is on our side!

Preparation For Translation   *Milton Crane*.................$ 7.95
This book is about YOUR preparation for translation. It is about YOUR plans to live without a mediator after probation closes. It is about God's plans for YOUR overcoming temptation NOW in anticipation of those events. It is about His plans for the renewing of YOUR mind through the final atonement ministry of Jesus. Spanish editions—$8.95.

Principles To Live By   *Mel Rees* ....$ 4.95
Dominion calls for individual decision and action—therefore, God gave man guiding principles to live by.

Quick-n-Easy Natural Recipes   *Lorrie Knutsen* ....$ 2.95
Every recipe has five or fewer ingredients and most take only minutes to prepare. Now you can enjoy simple, natural recipes without the drudgery!

Returning Back To Eden   *Betty-Ann Peters* ....$ 9.95
These recipes have been taste-tested by the world-wide travelers that have visited the Back to Eden Restaurant & Bakery in Minocqua, WI.

Right of the People   *A. T. Jones*....................................$11.95
This work, first printed in 1895, showed the relation that should exist between the church and state at the present time, as proved by Holy Writ and the historical evidence of twenty-five centuries

Rural Economy   *Ken LeBrun*...$ 2.50
"All that God's Word commands, we are to obey. All that it promises, we may claim. The life which it enjoins is the life that, through its power, we are to live."—Education, p. 188, 189.

The Savior Guides   *Alberta Wiggins* ....$ 8.95
The illustrations in this book assist the teacher to make this learning experience a delight for the young learners because it is compiled of drawings from among their peers and to furnish a complete lesson plan for the teacher who has limited time for preparation.

Sin Shall Not Have Dominion Over You   *C. Fitch*....$ 6.95
Fitch clarifies his position on sanctification and holiness by answering three questions: 1) Has God made provisions to save His people from their sins? 2) If so, can Christians avail themselves of it in this life? and 3) In what way may this provision become available? He uses the Bible as his only source to answer these questions.

Spurious Books of the Bible   *Gar Baybrook* ....$ 9.95
Compare the so-called Lost Books of the Bible with proven Scripture. Most have flagrant errors, some are tainted with pagan beliefs, while others are quite subtle in their claims.

Steps To Christ Study Guide   *Gail Bremner* ....$ 2.95
This study guide is designed to encourage the youth, and the young at heart, to understand and experience more fully a living relationship with Jesus.

Story of Daniel the Prophet   *S. N. Haskell* $11.95
This book especially applicable to our day: points out the immediate future and in its simplicity will attract many who might not be inclined to read deep, argumentative works. Facsimile Reprint.

Story of the Seer of Patmos   *S. N. Haskell* $12.95
The Book of Revelation pronounces a blessing upon everyone who reads it or hears it. This books gives the historic SDA view. Facsimile Reprint.

Stress: Taming the Tyrant   *Richard Neil* ....$ 8.95
Stress is an inevitable part of our 20th century lifestyle. Under the proper circumstances stress can be uplifting as well as depressing. It can either help us grow our hasten or death. Find out how to control, manage and modify stress.

Studies in Daniel and Revelation   *Kraid Ashbaugh*...$ 4.95
A convenient handbook containing paraphrases of EG White's comments after each verse in the books of Daniel & Revelation.

Studies in the Book of Hebrews   *E. J. Waggoner* ......$ 6.95
A series of studies given at the General Conference of 1897. The Bible studies that Elder Waggoner gave each day, are presented as live and full of hope for each Bible student today.

Subtle Challenge to God's Authority   *M. Crane*.......$ 5.50
Satan's deceptions are many and subtle. He has concentrated his attack on God's authority.

Such A Cloud of Witnesses   *Milton Crane* ....$ 4.95
You are called to be a witness for or against the government of God. Will your testimony help God or aid His enemy?

375 Meatless Recipes–CENTURY 21   *E. Nelson* .....$ 7.95
This book will help you learn how to feed your family in such a way that they will enjoy eating the foods that nutritionists tell us are an absolute must if we are going to make it into the twenty-first century.

Truth Triumphant *B. G. Wilkinson* $12.95
The history of God's true Church from Ireland, to the Waldenses, the struggle to preserve the Bible and the pure doctrine of the apostles is disclosed. Facsimile Reprint.

Understanding the Body Organs *Celeste Lee* ....$ 7.95
Simply and concisely explains how the body organs function and how they relate to one another. Also includes the eight laws of health, explaining each one and sharing many benefits that will be derived from following the entire plan.

Victory and Self-Mastery *J. N. Tindall*..........................$ 5.95
How Christ maintained a sinless character in a fallen, sinful, human nature. Facsimile Reprint.

Warning in Daniel 12 *Marian Berry*.............................$14.95
A study of the twelfth chapter of Daniel. It is warning we shall all need to understand before the end of time.

Who Killed Candida? *Vicki Glassburn* $17.95
Although diet is an important part of getting well, even the best food and supplements are undermined if you continue to unknowingly support yeast growth! The author will show you how making simple lifestyle choices can actually STOP THE YEAST SUPPORT CYCLE that other Candida programs do not address.

Whole Foods For Whole People *Lucy Fuller* $10.95
Whole Foods For Whole People is not just a cookbook, but a manual to teach people how they can live a longer, healthier lifestyle by using the natural resources which surround us.

The Word Was Made Flesh *Ralph Larson* ....$ 8.95
This book is on the human nature of Christ, with a limited, rather specialized objective. Dr. Larson does not deal directly with the whole issue of Christ's human nature. He traces the understanding of this aspect of Christology within the Seventh-day Adventist church from 1852–1952, providing a fairly comprehensive survey of historical data.

To order any of the above titles, see your local bookstore.

However, if you are unable to locate any title,
call 518/358-3652.